THE CLEARING IN THE WOODS

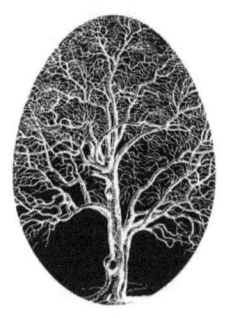

J.D. MATTHEWS

Copyright © J.D. Matthews, 2024
J.D. Matthews has asserted his right to be
identified as the author of this work.

All rights reserved.

No part of this publication may be reproduced,
stored in any retrieval system, or transmitted, in any form, or by any
means, electronic, mechanical, photocopying, recording, or
otherwise, without the prior written permission of the publishers.
This book is a work of fiction. Names, characters, businesses,
organizations, places and events, other than those clearly in the
public domain, are either the product of the author's imagination, or
are used fictitiously. Any resemblances to actual persons, living or
dead, events or locales are purely coincidental.

Cover design: Arjan van Woensel

Paperback ISBN: 978-1-7636179-0-2
eBook ISBN: 978-1-7636179-1-9

Contents

1. The Old Man — 1
2. The Young Man — 11
3. Unwelcome Guests — 21
4. Negotiations — 32
5. Flight — 47
6. Kyrubol — 59
7. A Rude Awakening — 72
8. The Dream — 84
9. The Stranger — 91
10. The Invitation — 97
11. The Girl — 106
12. The Four Daughters — 112
13. A Family Dinner — 120
14. Wife, Mother and Son — 130
15. Midnight Rendezvous — 143
16. Revelations — 152
17. Authentication — 162
18. Disappointment — 171
19. The Saviour — 180
20. Reunited — 193
21. Present Day — 201
22. A Parting Gift — 213

Acknowledgments — 223

The Old Man

"What's wrong, Tully?" I asked, stepping through the doorway into the bedroom. I headed towards the old man, coming to a stop at his bedside and pushed the stop button on the call bell.

"John, is it true?" asked Tully through his heavy accent, looking at me imploringly.

"Is what true?" I asked, frowning.

"Here, John, look here," said Tully excitedly, sitting up and picking up the newspaper from his bedside table before tapping on the headline on the front page.

"Dissolution of the Soviet Union, huh?" I read aloud with furrowed eyebrows. "As of Boxing Day. So, literally within the last forty-eight hours. Hey, that's big news, Tully! That's big enough I reckon it'll even push the cricket from the front page." And I gave him a sardonic smile.

"It's huge news, John, huge!" Replied Tully. "Yes! Finally! Russia is back!" He handed me the newspaper before clapping his hands together exuberantly. "I honestly didn't think I'd live to see it, John. You have no idea what it means to me to see the tricolour flying again," he finished, his face full of emotion.

"This is a cause for celebration, John. Would you care to join me?"

"Join you?" I asked in reply, confused.

"I know it's early but I thought, what the hell," he said, winking at me before leaning over the bed railing and opening his bedside cupboard drawer.

I looked on with confusion as the sounds of unseen belongings rattled around inside his drawer, before finally he withdrew his hand. "Nectar," I heard him triumphantly proclaim before revealing to me a three-quarters-full bottle of vodka. After repositioning himself on the bed, he held it up to show me. Finally understanding what he meant, my eyes met his which twinkled mischievously.

"Vodka?" I asked.

"The good stuff," he replied, his voice rising as a wide mischievous grin matching his eyes appeared upon his face.

"Ah, listen, Tully," I began reluctantly, a nervous grin crossing my own. "I can't when I'm on duty I'm afraid." I folded his newspaper in half before replacing it on his bedside table. The disappointment caused his grin to fade somewhat, so I relented. Besides, how could I say no to this pleasant old man? "Um, at the end of my shift however, sure, why not? I'd be delighted too."

And his face lit up again, the mischievous grin now replaced by a broad warm smile. He placed the bottle of vodka on his table. "That's fine, John, perfectly fine. I'm more than happy to wait until then."

"But just one, Tully," I interjected, staring him straight in the eye. "I have to be able to drive home, remember." He nodded in understanding although his mischievous grin had quickly returned and was deceiving. Alas, I knew better but despite this I couldn't help but chuckle again at this animated old man.

"Would you like to hear a story, John?" he asked me, suddenly becoming serious. "Perhaps later whilst we share our drink?" he added with a questioning look.

"A story huh?" I replied, intrigued. "What kind of story?"

"A story from home," he replied softly. "A story from my home in Russia," he added, adding emphasis to the second sentence and immediately adding to my intrigue. He never spoke about his life in Russia. In fact, beyond a couple of titbits, nobody knew anything at all about it, myself included. I looked at him, searching his now impassive face for answers.

We both eyed the other in silence for a few moments, me in breathless anticipation of further possible revelations and him patiently waiting for me to enquire. Just as the silence became uncomfortable, that warm smile reappeared as easily and quickly as it had disappeared a few moments earlier and he waved his hand dismissively.

"It's more than obvious to me, John, that you would like to hear my story," Tully stated with satisfaction.

"I certainly would, Tully," I replied, nodding enthusiastically. "You do realise you're a bit of a mystery to us here at the home? A novelty even? One of these enigmas wrapped in a riddle." This revelation must have pleased him because he nodded his head enthusiastically in agreement.

"How long have you lived here now? How long have I been nursing you? Ten years, give or take? Most residents will chew your ear off at the slightest provocation but not you. So, yes please, I would love to hear any or all of the stories you would like to tell!" And I patted his shoulder reassuringly.

"Excellent, excellent. I just wanted to make certain, John," said Tully, smiling appreciatively.

"But dare I ask, Tully? What kind of story is it?" I asked hesitantly.

To my question, he looked away, turning his head to stare

directly out through his window and become lost in thought. A moment later, he turned back to me and cleared his throat. Finally, he spoke.

"Let's just say, it's the kind an old man would tell to his grandson." He said, and our eyes locked. I couldn't help but notice his had become watery, almost as if they were on the precipice of tears.

Before I replied, A feeling of appreciation and gratitude washed over me mixed with a combination of discomfort and awkwardness. "Well, I'm touched you feel that way, Tully, genuinely. You know I do enjoy your company."

"John, I can't express my gratitude to you enough for bringing your children in to visit me yesterday," he said shakily. "It was such a wonderful and unexpected Christmas present."

"You're welcome," I replied, momentarily absent of any further discourse, so I simply flashed him an appreciative smile.

"You know I have no family here in Australia, or in Russia for that matter," he said, repeating one of the few things I knew about him before following it with another. "That bastard Stalin saw to that," he added, that snippet of information rife with bitterness and spat out like poison. To which I didn't know what to say so I simply shook my head in quiet reservation.

Meanwhile, Tully watched me intently before reaching up to take my hand in his. "It's okay, Tully," I said reassuringly, feeling his rough palm in mine and patting his forearm with my free hand. "How about I get you a coffee? Would you like a coffee?" I asked, nodding my head suggestively in part with hopes of changing the subject. "I know how much you Russians love your coffee. Which begs the question, which one do you love more? Coffee or vodka?" I asked, winking at him and flashing a cheeky grin.

"Sadly, these days it's coffee, John, and yes, I would love one please," he replied with enthusiasm. "Black as usual please. You know, I'm feeling pretty tired today. The excitement at the demise of the Bolsheviks must have taken it out of me," he said as he released my hand and laid himself back onto his bed gently before resting his head on his pillow. "Maybe after lunch I'll have a little sleep. Ensure I'm running on full batteries for our drink later."

"I think that's a terrific idea, Tully," I said brightly, watching him as he wriggled himself down into a more comfortable position. "Now you know my shift doesn't finish until three p.m., so you've got plenty of time before then. I'll go make that coffee for you now but when I come back, I've got to get back to work."

"Of course, John, of course, I understand. Thank you," replied Tully, smiling warmly. "I apologise if I've held you up."

"That's okay, Tully, you've done nothing of the sort. Don't hesitate to hit your call bell if you need something," I said reassuringly.

I exited the room and headed straight for the kitchenette. Within five minutes I'd prepared his coffee and returned to his room only to find him sound asleep. I placed the cup down gently on his bedside table and found myself rereading the headline on the newspaper which now rested across his chest. He grasped it by one hand and it rose and fell slowly in rhythm with every breath. I took particular notice of the Russian tricolour flag flying over the Kremlin and read the description under the front-page photograph: "Soviet hammer and sickle flag lowered for the last time over the Kremlin."

It wasn't embellishing when I said that the other nurses and I knew next to nothing about this mysterious Russian man, his medical record notwithstanding. His personal life, both current and past, was a complete mystery, and I'd known him ten years.

At first, he hadn't been particularly outgoing. However, once he'd become comfortable with myself and others, he'd begun to exhibit an increasing level of outward warmth. I sensed that, despite this, he always remained wary, and far more interested in learning about our lives than sharing anything from his own.

The headline and his reaction intrigued me. He had obviously emigrated to Australia sometime between the first and second World Wars, the first of which he'd served in. How do I know this, you might ask? He'd lost family members during Stalin's reign, a fact that he had disclosed more than once over the years and remained bitter at. Also, his medical record had disclosed the type of traumatic injuries that many veterans obtained.

I watched the man curiously for a moment, smiling to myself at how peaceful he looked as he slept. It struck me then just how much this man had seen and done in his life. Instantaneously, a myriad of questions exploded into my mind.

What potential world-altering events had he witnessed? What were his experiences of war? How had he been injured? Where had it happened? What was the Russia he remembers like? What were his thoughts about the Romanovs, the Russian Revolution, Vladimir Lenin and Joseph Stalin? Well, I suspected I knew the answer to the last one.

I realise we're all only a blip on the map but therein lies my curiosity. Life isn't linear. We share time with billions of others on this planet but the vast majority of our lives won't intersect, instead running parallel and remaining so until the day one of us dies. And there I go again, waxing philosophical and delving into existentialism...

Tully was suffering from Alzheimer's, although he had only recently been diagnosed. Considering his age – he'd turned ninety-three years old the month before – he was faring well. After all, he was still able to walk, granted it was with a cane or walker, and still fed and showered himself.

"Hey John," came my colleague's voice through the doorway, causing me to jump and re-enter reality. "I need a hand with Bill."

I took my eyes off Tully and turned around to find David's head poking around the door.

"If you've got a minute, that is?" asked David with a serious look. "Is everything okay?"

Collecting my thoughts, I took a moment to respond. "Um, yeah sure mate. And yeah, everything's fine." I started towards the door but stopped to look back as I passed through it. Tully remained asleep.

I visited Tully's room several more times during the day but upon each visit he was either eating or sleeping so I didn't disturb him. The end of my shift arrived and keeping my word I returned.

Upon entering his room, I was pleasantly surprised to find him seated beside his window in his leather armchair and waiting for me expectantly. He looked up as I entered and his face broke into a smile to rival that of the Cheshire cat. Perhaps it was the angle of the setting sun or the reflections through the glass, but I thought to myself as I drew nearer that he looked younger than I'd ever seen him look before.

"John," he said affectionately. "Come and sit down, my friend." He enthusiastically motioned towards the upholstered leather armchair across from him. Between us sat a small wooden table upon which rested two small glasses and in between them, the bottle of vodka.

Once I'd taken my seat, I sat back and watched as he carefully poured a generous portion of vodka into one glass before looking up at me inquisitively. "Half of that for me please," I said, smiling in response to the unasked question. I observed his face more closely as he leaned over to pour. It was awash with enjoyment and bathed in an almost angelic if not ethereal light that was coming through the window from the setting sun.

"There is a phrase in Russian that is similar to your Australian saying of cheers," Tully stated, sitting back after replacing the lid on the vodka and placing the bottle back down on the table between us. "If you'll kindly repeat after me John." And he raised his glass into the air. "Nah-zda-rovh-yeh."

"Nah-zda-rovh-yeh," I replied uncertainly, hopeful that I hadn't butchered the pronunciation. I raised my glass into the air, where it was met with a loud clink by Tully's, who then proceeded to down his entire portion in one swallow.

I sat there both surprised and impressed. "Wow, Tully, you've really been holding out for that drink," I chuckled. "Here I was thinking you'd forgotten," I added, while he simply smiled at me before pouring himself a second glass and repeating the process.

"You must know by now John that Russians never forget," he replied with amusement. "Are you not going to drink yours?"

"No, no, I'll drink it alright, although I'll think I'll sip mine, thanks," I replied jovially. "Besides, you mentioned a story and I'd kind of like to be awake to hear it and sober enough to remember it."

"Yes, yes, that's correct, John," he replied, chuckling as he placed his glass down before clapping his hands together again. "You are still interested in hearing it then?"

"Of course, Tully. That's why I'm here. That and of course the company," I added quickly, nodding affectionately and raising my glass to toast him.

"Excellent, excellent," Tully said, eyes twinkling. "I think you'll enjoy this story, John," he added before refilling his glass for a third time.

"What's it about again? And is it a true story?" I asked.

"Well John, that's the tricky part. It's entirely up to the listener to decide," he replied, mysteriously.

Looking at him curiously, I raised my eyebrows. Despite observing my expression, Tully allowed several seconds to pass without any elaboration so I decided to ask. "And what does that mean?" His reply? Little more than a cagey smile. "Okay then, what's the setting?" I asked, moving on but all the more intrigued.

"The height of summer in Siberia in Soviet Russia. The year? 1923. The civil war has only recently ended," he replied with a surprising intensity. "A young man, a veteran of the Great War and the Russian Revolution, takes a walk in the woods one day. From there the following tale unfolds," he added, finishing the sentence by draining his glass of vodka for a third time.

"Maybe you should take it easy on that stuff?" I asked with concern. "Remember, you're on medication. A little's okay but not a lot, okay?"

He smiled at me, a simple yet grateful smile. "One more, John, and I'm done. I promise," he said, pouring himself a fourth and hopefully final glass of vodka. Meanwhile, I hadn't even touched mine.

"Drink your vodka, John," he said, looking at my still full

glass. "And I will begin," he added, before I picked up my glass and sipped. The vodka burning as it went down my throat.

After a brief coughing fit, I lifted my glass into the air and once again toasted my elderly friend. "Jeez, that stuff's strong, Tully. But very well, you may begin."

The Young Man

He crouched down behind a low stone wall, pressing himself as hard as he could to it to conceal himself from the enemy's gunfire. Bullets flew all around him, their unmistakable sound almost deafening. One ricocheted across the top of the wall directly above him and only inches from his head. He forced himself, if it was possible, even lower to the ground and his hands and knees further into the thick mud.

In the rare and infrequent moments when his ears were not filled with the sounds from the battle raging all around him, they were filled instead with the anguished cries of his comrades as they were being torn apart, felled by bullets and shell blasts. He'd found early on that he preferred the sound of gunfire.

"Vitaly!" yelled his comrade from behind. He too was pressed agonisingly close to the stone wall and could easily have rested his chin on the man in front's shoulder, such was their close proximity.

"Vitaly!" yelled the man again, directly into his comrade's ear this time, ensuring he would be heard. A shell burst nearby, causing mud, soil and stone to rain down upon them in a torrential downpour. It completely covered them, momentarily obscuring light and sound and preventing coherent thought.

"We must keep moving!" the man yelled, coughing up dust and dirt and spitting it out on the ground. The man in front nodded his understanding, then mustering every ounce of courage he possessed, he sprang up. Resting his rifle on the top of the stone wall, he fired off several quick rounds. Whether he hit anything, he didn't know. You didn't wait and look around.

His comrade sprang out from behind him and fired off several rounds of his own. As the last shell casing ejected from his rifle, he turned and ran as fast as his legs would carry him. His destination was only a few metres away where more comrades were taking cover behind a felled tree, their voices inaudible over the sounds of the raging battle but their aspirations clear. It was time to advance and they waved frantically for their comrades to join them.

Then time slowed. About half way between cover his comrade stopped and turned, reacting instinctively to the cry of pain. It was in that instance, in that microsecond of indecision where he met his fate. People do foolish things in war. They say fortune favours the brave. Does that mean misfortune favours the cowardly? This man was no coward. A fool, perhaps, but to be foolish is human nature. Then there came an almighty boom and he was killed.

It had been Vitaly who'd cried out and caused the distraction that would inadvertently cost his comrade his life. An action that would become a great source of regret that he would frequently revisit over the years to come. He had risen up in readiness to sprint after his comrade when a bullet had grazed his left knuckle. Surprised and in pain, all he could do was watch as the shell hit.

Cradling his injured hand, he looked up just in time to

meet his comrade's eye. One last look, one last thought, one last moment of understanding between them before he was vaporised into a red mist before his very eyes. However bad witnessing that was, worse yet was being covered in it. Then he fell to the ground, no longer able to stand and not understanding why.

As the dust and dirt slowly cleared, realisation washed over him. He looked down to discover his leg was gone, torn to shreds by the same blast that had obliterated his comrade. Panic rising, he began to scream as he sat there watching the blood pour out from the wound and soak the ground beneath him.

He grabbed at his stump in shock, rational thought having left his mind. This was it, he thought. This is where I'm going to die. He frantically reached down and clumsily felt around for his knee. Finding it, he begun moving lower and found shin, then ankle and finally his foot. What sweet relief! It was all still there, he silently thanked God, although it was still severely damaged.

Suddenly a comrade grabbed him under the arms and dragged him back behind the safety of the stone wall. There, with the assistance of another, they applied pressure until a medic could reach them. They screamed panicked instructions to each other in between reassurances to their injured comrade. Then suddenly he stirred and woke.

Another night, another nightmare. It was a continuous vicious cycle. He straightened out his leg which cracked loudly in response, but alas it was still there. He often checked, just to be sure, for he sometimes lost track of where dreams finished and reality began.

He opened his eyes to a lightless room and looked out through the window at the darkness beyond. A faint light came from behind the heavy curtain that acted as a partition to his corner of the izba. He could hear movement beyond, indicating that his parents were awake and likely preparing breakfast in anticipation of another hard day of ploughing the fields. He could smell coffee, bread and the leftover stew from their dinner the evening before. His stomach growled.

He sat up and dropped his legs over the edge of his cot. Taking hold of the frame, he swung his right leg back and forth slowly, loosening the joint up in the process but causing him to grimace in pain. He realised he was coated in sweat and shivered despite the unusual warmth in the morning air.

"Are you awake, Vitaly?" came his mother's firm voice from behind the curtain.

He remained silent, wiping his brow with his forearm before extending his arms above him and causing several of his bones to crack as he stretched out.

"Vitaly?" came her voice again, this time more pressing. He wasn't ready to face her yet – his father either, or the world for that matter. He knew however that she wouldn't be ignored for long and would soon be tearing back the curtain regardless. Lena was like that. She was what you would call no nonsense.

"Yes, Mama," he replied sleepily.

"Breakfast is ready," came a sharp reply. "Get up and eat so you can get out there and help your father. It's already warm and it's only going to get warmer," she added.

Vitaly groaned in response, carefully though so his mother wouldn't hear him. He leaned over and clumsily opened the bottom drawer of his bureau and began rummaging inside. A few seconds later he withdrew a beaten old silver flask, unscrewed the lid and gulped down a large mouthful. "Ahh," he said with a great sigh. Satisfied, he placed the flask back on the bureau but left the lid unscrewed.

He rose stiffly then began fumbling around in the dark for his clothes before conceding defeat and lighting a candle.

Bathed in the soft flickering light he dressed himself clumsily, unaware he'd put his pants on backwards until he couldn't find the fly. Correcting his mistake, he sat back down on his cot to put on his shoes before standing up again and stepping over to the wash basin to splash some water on his face.

He looked into the mirror above the basin and paused to observe his own reflection. Staring back at him was a handsome twenty-four-year-old Russian man. He stood six feet tall and was of a lean yet muscular build. His hair was jet black and short cropped with a matching moustache and goatee. His eyes were dark green and serious. He'd experienced a lot in his short life. War, revolution, tragedy and injury. All these factors combined to make him, at least spiritually, a much older man. He reached again for the flask and took another shot then hastily brushed his teeth.

"Come, Vitaly," came his mother's voice again, more forceful this time having finally lost her patience. Her rapid footsteps approached and suddenly the curtain was torn open aggressively. Vitaly was quick though. He had replaced the lid and dropped the flask back into the open bureau drawer and shut it with a firm nudge from his hip. Looking up, he shielded his eyes from the bright light now flooding his space as his mother stared back at him with a stern look upon her face.

"Mama, please!" he cried with exasperation.

"Please nothing," replied his mother dismissively whilst wagging a threatening finger at him. "You need to get up, eat your breakfast and get out there and help your father," she added.

"Okay, Mama, okay," he responded defensively as he hurriedly moved past her whilst carefully avoiding her eye.

He dropped into his chair at the kitchen table and poured himself a large mug of steaming hot coffee. He savoured that first delicious mouthful before quickly wolfing down his breakfast. No time to saviour it though, he thought – if he lingered even momentarily his mother would start in on him again.

"You'll find your father down in the middle field," his mother began. "he's been up since five and you've gone and overslept," she said with annoyance before continuing to ramble to herself. "I thought we were done with these requisitions once the war ended yet Karasev, or at least his men, continue to visit us every month and take our produce."

Vitaly, mouth full, replied simply with a non-committal grunt.

"What do the people in Petrograd and Moscow know of suffering?" she continued. "What do they know about life here in Virubol or any other village or Siberia for that matter? I thought things were meant to be better under Bolshevism," she exclaimed bitterly.

Vitaly swallowed another mouthful and followed it with another sip from his coffee before deciding to answer. "I don't know, Mama," he said, shrugging his shoulders carelessly. His response didn't placate her; instead, she launched into another rambling diatribe.

"It's hard to fathom that he's the same boy I taught," she said bitterly as she shook her head in disapproval.

"Karasev's okay, Mama," stated Vitaly reassuringly, leaning back in his chair. "After all, he's only doing his job," he added.

"Yes, I understand that," she replied shortly, pulling out a chair and taking a seat across from her son. "I remember when that boy was timid and afraid of his own shadow. Bolshevism has obviously done wonders for him," she added sarcastically.

"He can be reasoned with," said Vitaly through another mouthful of his breakfast.

"Reason? That boy can't comprehend reason. He's a fool!"

"I'll talk to him and explain our circumstances. He'll

understand," Vitaly said confidently, his mother looking on stony-faced.

"He wouldn't listen to your father so what makes you think he'll listen to you?"

"Because we were both Bolsheviks, Mama. And, letters don't convey tone." explained Vitaly, matter of fact.

At the mention of his own connection to Bolshevism, his mother's demeanour softened considerably and she even smiled a rare yet understanding smile. She hadn't always been like this. War and revolution had changed her. It had changed everyone. She reached her hand out across the table and patted the top of Vitaly's softly.

"Yes, I know, Vitaly," she said softly. "You know I love you, don't you?" she asked tentatively as tears appeared in her eyes.

"Of course, I know, Mama," replied Vitaly reassuringly, turning over his hand and taking his mothers in his lovingly. "Please don't cry."

"We're hard on you I know," she stated, implicating herself and his father by nodding in the direction of the middle field. "Understand it's because I'm scared for you. So many boys have come back from the war damaged. You more than most, at least physically."

"I understand, Mama," he replied, squeezing her hand.

"If I just keep you busy, keep you on working, I think to myself, then you'll be okay," she explained before looking away, her lips trembling as she suppressed the urge to cry.

"You don't need to worry about me, Mama," stated Vitaly firmly. "I've survived two wars," he added proudly. "And all before the age of twenty-five!" He gave her a wry smile.

"Yes, I know, Vitaly. I also know that you suffer," she said softly, looking him in the eye. Vitaly's expression was quizzical. "And that you drink — which I can only presume is to lessen your suffering," she added timidly, fearful at the possible reactions to her statement.

Vitaly let go of his mother's hand and stared into her eyes, gauging her demeanour and deciding how best to respond. Knowing better than to lie to her, he instead went on the offensive. "How do you know?"

"I've seen you drink, Vitaly. And I smell it on your breath. I've also found more than one of your flasks that you'd thought you'd hidden so cleverly around the farm," she replied sheepishly whilst flashing him an understanding smile. "And you sometimes talk in your sleep," she added.

He suddenly felt ashamed, weak and powerless. Yes, he had stashed several flasks filled with vodka around the farm and often carried another on his person. As for talking in his sleep, he knew to what she referred. The bad dreams. How should he handle this? he thought to himself.

"Don't worry about me, Mama, okay?" he replied dismissively. "Yes, I cannot deny that I do enjoy the occasional vodka but I don't let it..."

"Don't let it what?" she interjected sharply, her demeanour rapidly changing again. "You're often drunk. Your father and I notice. If not every night, then almost every night!"

"No, I am not, Mama!" he replied with attitude, his voice rising.

"Oh, no?" she asked sarcastically. "Then tell me, Vitaly, what is it you dream about at night?"

With a combative smirk, Vitaly replied, "You wouldn't understand, Mama."

To this statement her expression changed yet again. Vitaly suspected she might start crying and immediately felt guilty. He knew that look. He'd seen it before, inflicted it before. It was one of heartbreak. Although she tried valiantly to mask it.

"I'm sorry, Mama," he said softly, quickly correcting

himself and reaching out and taking her hand again. "But the truth is, you wouldn't understand. Couldn't understand," he added.

"Then talk to me, please! Explain it! Make me understand!" she implored. "Please! Let me and your father in. Let us unburden your heavy shoulders," she added, her eyes filling with tears as they sat there and looked across at each other.

"No, Mama, I don't think I will," replied Vitaly defiantly. He again felt ashamed. He knew she only wanted to help but the only people who would understand were his comrades who had fought in the war. "Remember, Karasev is only the front man for these requisitions and that he answers to someone else. Now I don't know who that someone is but I know Karasev. He'll listen to me," explained Vitaly, quickly changing the subject. His mother looked on, sad and defeated before she wiped her eyes with the side of her hand.

As they sat there, the room had been growing slowly brighter, the sun's rays breaking through the far trees and bathing their empty wheat fields in its early morning light. Vitaly was flooded with admiration. Far off down the field he could see his father toiling away at his thankless task. And for what? Just to have it taken away.

"And what are you going to say to him?" his mother asked.

"I'll explain to him that Papa is proud and won't accept any help unless it's yours or mine." Vitaly pointed to his mother and then himself. "Despite obviously needing more help than you or I can offer. He's getting older and his body's breaking down."

"And suppose he doesn't accept that?"

"They took the farm when they nationalised everything so it's their job to find and provide help," Vitaly explained. "The problem is, Papa still thinks he owns the farm, still treats it accordingly and I can't blame him. His father was born and grew up under serfdom before finally being able to farm his own land. This land. Karasev can't ignore that sentimentality is involved."

"And if he does, Vitaly? Then what?"

Vitaly exhaled loudly before pursing his lips and shaking his head slowly from side to side. "I don't know, Mama. I wouldn't underestimate our local Soviet though. If Papa doesn't acquiesce to their demands, they'll likely arrest him."

His mother stared at him with wide eyes that were full of worry. He released her hand before gently patting it again. Smiling at her, he rose and rounded the table to embrace her warmly and plant a kiss on her cheek. "It'll be okay, Mama," he said, reassuringly. "Trust me," he added, stepping away and winking at her. "Now I suppose I should go and help Papa."

He walked towards the door, stopping just inside to remove his tobacco pouch and cap from the coat rack. After grabbing his canteen and ensuring it was full, he opened the door before turning back to look again at his mother. He smiled reassuringly at her. "Remember, Mama, it'll be okay," he said before pulling the door closed behind him. However, deep down, he knew that that mightn't be true. Sadly, the Bolsheviks had them between a rock and a hard place.

Unwelcome Guests

Vitaly pulled his cap down firmly over his head as he stepped outside to what was a beautiful morning on the Western Siberian Plain. He pulled a pre-rolled cigarette from inside his tobacco pouch and removed a match from his pants pocket and lit it. He inhaled deeply as he took a moment to take in the ambiance. The sun was rising fast now and as his mother had stated, the morning was already considerably warm and only going to get warmer. It was unusual weather considering even in the depths of summer it was not uncommon for it to still drop below freezing overnight.

He descended the stairs briskly with cigarette in mouth and his right knee clicking noisily. He turned right round the side of the izba before passing through the cobbled farm yard. He inspected the different buildings as he passed and counted the number of pumpkins growing in the garden. Being from the peasant class, his family didn't possess, nor could they afford, the latest and most advanced equipment necessary for farming. They did however engage in subsistence farming and were therefore self-reliant and sustainable.

The layout of the farm was simple. It included three big fields that ran off into the distance from the izba while the front, where he now stood, was met by the gravel road that would take you into the village of Virubol. At the immediate back of the izba and before the middle field stood the family's barn and small dairy, a chicken pen and small kitchen garden that was abundant with an assortment of staple vegetables. There was also a well that supplied drinking water and a banya used for sweat bathing.

They owned two horses which completed the bulk of the farm's considerable labour including all of the ploughing, sowing and harvesting and which were at this moment down in the field with his father. There were two cows for milk and cheese and a dozen chickens for eggs and occasionally eating. They had a cat called Tizzy to keep the mouse and rat population under control and his father had a Russian wolfhound called Lex, named after Czar Alexander II.

As he crossed the yard, he tripped over one of the chickens, causing him to drop his cigarette, tobacco pouch and canteen. Swearing loudly, he regained his balance and picked up his dropped possessions before swinging his leg wildly at the chook in frustration. He brushed off his cigarette and placed it back in his mouth then dusted himself off and continued towards the gate.

His father had forbidden smoking in the fields so he stopped on the inside of the gate and took several deep drags on his cigarette. He observed the field in front of him which had a section roped off from the others to contain their cows. After a final drag, he crushed out his cigarette against the gate post and dropped it to the ground before stepping through and closing the gate behind himself and walking down the undulating field towards his father in the distance.

At a brisk walk, it still took several minutes for Vitaly to reach his father, who had spotted him coming. Vitaly's father, Pyotr, had decided to stop for a quick drink break while he awaited his son's imminent arrival. He had removed his cap and was wiping his sweaty brow when he greeted his only son.

"Good morning, Vitaly. Awfully nice of you to join me," he added sarcastically.

"Good morning, Pyotr. I mean Papa," replied Vitaly in kind, with a cheeky smirk before shaking his head with amusement. This was their relationship. Casual but respectful. "How's the ploughing going?" he asked as he bent down and patted Lex affectionately.

"Not too bad," his father replied whilst ignoring his son's sarcasm. "The ground's a bit dry but that's to be expected with this heat."

"When do you expect to start sowing?" asked Vitaly seriously.

"In a few weeks. Maybe six, maybe eight," he replied with uncertainty before drinking again from his canteen. "It's a big job and I'll need your help again, just like with the harvest." he added, searching his son's face.

"I'll be here Papa, just like with the harvest." He replied with resignation. "How are the horses holding up?" And he walked over to the pair and patted them affectionately. His father always carried a small pouch with him that contained a few carrots that he would give them as a reward for their hard work. The pouch was on the ground in front of them so Vitaly reached down and opened it and withdrew two bright orange ones.

"I was just about to do that myself," stated his father, "and they're well."

After dropping his canteen to the ground, Vitaly rested a carrot in his open palm and held it up to the first horse, who chomped into it enthusiastically and made it quickly disappear. He then placed the other carrot in his open palm and repeated the process with the second horse before patting them both gently on their crests.

"How was your mother this morning?" enquired Pyotr sheepishly as he gave his son a searching look.

"The usual," replied Vitaly with a shrug of the shoulders. He understood what that look meant. It indicated to Vitaly that his father knew of the conversation he'd just had with his mother and the topic they'd discussed. "She needs to go back to teaching though. All of this isolation is making her crazy."

"She worries," stated Pyotr firmly. "She worries about everything. You, me, the farm."

"She definitely worries about you," stated Vitaly, staring at his father intently.

"She thinks I'm going to get arrested," said Pyotr with a chuckle. "And the local Soviet is going to throw me in the Gulag."

"It is possible," said Vitaly, smiling, although deep down he was worried too. He knew his father wouldn't surrender control of the farm easily. "What time is Karasev arriving again? And more importantly, what are you going to do when he gets here?"

"Nine is what the letter said and honestly, my boy, I don't know. I've left my rifle in the izba for a reason," he replied, sadness evident in his voice. "I don't intend to give my farm up to some fucking Bolshevik though," he added with bitterness whilst flipping his hat over in his hands.

"You won't be giving it up though, Papa, not really," Vitaly explained almost pleadingly. "Yes, under nationalisation you lose ownership but the local Soviet still need someone to run it, harvest the grain, milk the cows, collect the eggs and so on. It's in their own best interest to leave the actual day to day running of the farm under your control."

"Sounds like serfdom to me, son. I farm the land for someone else's gain? Your grandfather grew up under that system on this very farm. Told me stories about it," stated Pyotr with passion. "I won't be the one to lose the first farm our family ever owned!"

"It's not serfdom and you won't be losing it, Papa! The way you'll lose it is by losing your temper and telling the Soviet to get fucked and not cooperating with them."

"I don't care, Vitaly!" Pyotr replied defiantly, anger rising in his voice.

"You realise, under nationalism the Soviets will supply you with workers to help with the harvest?" Vitaly said, his voice also rising.

"I don't need any help!" replied Pyotr loudly. "When you ran off and joined the army your mother and I managed just fine and you and your mother are worth ten of Karasev!" he stated passionately.

Vitaly stood there and looked at his father almost pityingly. He had always been stubborn and proud. Traits he had passed down to Vitaly. Is pride worth losing your home over though? he thought to himself. Surely not. He felt defeated, so, lowering his voice, he decided to offer his father one more piece of advice.

"Papa," he began softly. "You do whatever it is you think you have to but be warned, those who don't go along and dance to the Bolsheviks' tune suffer at their hands regardless of their transgressions. Do you want to get arrested and thrown in jail? What about Mama? They'll likely throw her in prison too."

He continued, "Do yourself a favour and accept their terms. I have! We're beaten here and it's foolish to resist," he finished, all the while hating himself for saying these things.

His father gave him a look he recognised. It was

disappointment and it hurt Vitaly to see it. His father held his gaze and Vitaly didn't dare look away.

"I've had my taste of freedom and independence I'm afraid," stated Pyotr calmly. "I'd rather rot in prison than willingly surrender my farm, my home, my life. We made it through the war when you were away. We survived the war communism that was enforced upon us. And do you want to know how we did it?"

"How, Papa?"

"We knew then that what was being taken was being given to millions of young men just like you. Therefore, we wanted to contribute, needed to contribute. Our conscience wouldn't have allowed us to sleep at night if we hadn't. But now? I don't support the fucking Bolsheviks!" He spat. "Not after what they did to this country!"

There would be no persuading him, conceded Vitaly finally, now genuinely scared. Scared for his mother and father, Pyotr and Lena Borisov, and how they would through Pyotr's own stubbornness lose their farm and be forced to either go into exile or be arrested and imprisoned. And what would he do? He shuddered to think about it.

"Listen. Would you forget about Brest-Litovsk for one moment? It's a done deal Papa," he said with frustration. His father habitually brought the subject up and although he hadn't mentioned it just now specifically, Vitaly knew it was what he was referring to.

"Forget?" his father shot back savagely. "Ukraine, Belarus, Lithuania, Latvia, Estonia and more all carved up and gifted to those fucking Germans. I suppose though I should be grateful?" he asked sarcastically. "At least they had the decency to surrender and then subsequently get screwed themselves. Not that they didn't deserve it! My respect for the French grew exponentially with the treaty of

Versailles," he finished, smiling to himself with satisfaction.

Father and son stood in silence as Pyotr slowly regained his composure. After several deep breaths he looked at his son. "Sorry, Vitaly," he stated softly. "My frustrations are not directed at you, obviously."

"I know, Papa," replied Vitaly soothingly and he stepped towards his father and patted him gently on his shoulder.

"I don't know, Papa, between you and Mama," Vitaly stated, slowly shaking his head.

"What don't you know?" asked Pyotr, confused.

"Who makes me drink more," replied Vitaly with a cheeky smile.

His father laughed as his son put his arm around his shoulders and gave him an affectionate squeeze before kissing him lightly on the forehead.

Pulling away, Pyotr replied playfully, "Just for that, you can finish the ploughing yourself."

Vitaly laughed again before crouching down to pet Lex. The wolfhound had been watching his masters with intense curiosity as they had had their exchange. Meanwhile, the two horses watched on nonchalantly.

"Sorry, Lex," said Pyotr, patting his pant leg encouragingly before Lex jumped up. He sniffed his master's hand eagerly before Pyotr patted him and told him what a good boy he was.

"Would you actually mind finishing off the last few rows, Vitaly?" asked Pyotr. "I don't think I can. The heat's gotten to me I'm afraid," he added, face bright red as he swallowed another mouthful of water from his canteen before pouring some over his head and face. Vitaly watched as it dripped down onto his shirt and ground before replying.

"Sure, Papa." He stepped back to the two horses and gave them another pet before taking up his position on the plough behind them. The plough was bulky, heavy and awkward but was the key reason, at least in Vitaly's mind, for his considerable physical upper body strength. He'd been working on it for years. Ever since he was a small boy.

His father still watched him like a hawk as he worked. He'd stand over there silently critiquing his work. It'd been the same his whole life. His father meant no harm, he was merely a perfectionist. A trait that came with private ownership and pride being taken in one's personal property. Yes, Vitaly wasn't looking forward to Karasev's imminent arrival.

The distraction of work didn't help Vitaly either. Usually, days spent in the field either sowing and harvesting were followed by the soundest night's sleep he'd had since returning from the Eastern Front. At least he had that to look forward to, he thought to himself. But where would he be sleeping tonight? In his cot in the izba or a jail cell with his parents besides him?

An hour or so passed before Vitaly completed his arduous task. He'd lost track of time and how many times he'd gone up and down the fields. A myriad of thoughts had distracted him, bouncing around his mind. Looking up, he found his father waving at him and motioning for him to join him. Looking further afield, he realised why. Karasev and his entourage had arrived and were standing with his mother inside the back gate waiting for them. They were early.

He guided the plough and horses back to his father, collected their belongings, and started back for the farm yard and izba. They walked in silence with the horses and Lex, his father leading while Vitaly drove the plough carefully so the great steel blade didn't cut a great long divot up the paddock. With a final ominous look at each other, they reached the back gate and looked up at their guests.

"Comrades Borisov," came Boris Karasev's unpleasant

voice. He reached over the top of the gate to shake Pyotr's hand, then followed it with Vitaly's. Both father and son were sorely tempted to crush his hand in theirs but resisted. As if sensing this, Karasev flashed them a knowing smile before stepping back and allowing them through the gate and into the yard.

Stepping through the gate, Vitaly observed Karasev and the three men accompanying him. Karasev was the only one he knew and could be described as weedy. He stood about five foot seven inches tall and was of a slight build. He had short brown hair with dark grey eyes and possessed a distinctively high-pitched voice which rose even higher when he was excited.

There were maybe two months between them in age, Vitaly being the older, and he recalled them being occasional childhood playmates. Despite this, he had often teased Karasev for his high-pitched voice and often called him a girl. The Karasev family were bakers in Virubol but had relocated to Ekaterinburg during the Civil War where the father, Kirill, had died unexpectedly.

Upon closer inspection, Vitaly found one of the other three men to be vaguely familiar. He was a bear of a man, an almost humorous opposite of Karasev. He stood about six foot four inches tall with broad shoulders and thick torso. His face was an emotionless mask of impassiveness with a hint of boredom. Vitaly guessed he had a shaved head concealed under his cap that would undoubtedly match his jet-black eyebrows. The man noticed Vitaly eyeing him curiously and matched his gaze for a moment before acknowledging him with the slightest of nods.

The other two were completely unfamiliar, indistinctive and unremarkable in anyway and easily forgettable even in an empty room, Vitaly thought. Why it required four men for this meeting Vitaly didn't know. He could understand maybe two. Perhaps Karasev accompanied by this silent, bored giant? If nothing else, he was intimidating.

"If you could allow us a few minutes, Boris, we'll get our horses and equipment packed away and join you inside," said Pyotr with forced conviviality. "My wife Lena – you know Lena? – will take care of you," he added, pointing to her as he spoke.

"Thank you, comrade and yes, we have just become reacquainted," Karasev replied pleasantly. "Although there was no need. I remember Mrs Borisov fondly from my school days when I shared a classroom with Vitaly here." He turned to look at Vitaly as he said it and smiled. Vitaly responded in kind but it was forced and insincere.

Karasev mustn't have noticed for he turned away and began looking around with pleasant curiosity before turning back to them and nodding approvingly. "Your hospitality is very much appreciated. But I must instruct you, from this moment on in our interactions you are to refer to me as Comrade Karasev." He smiled smugly. Vitaly suddenly found himself in agreement with his mother. How was this the same Boris Karasev? The same little weed his mother had taught and he had attended school with?

"Ah, would you like to come inside?" asked Lena reluctantly to the group of men.

"Certainly," replied Karasev, nodding his approval again while the three men accompanying him remained silent. "But please Mrs Borisov, ladies first," he said politely, waving his arm in faux exuberance to let her pass.

Lena chanced a worried look back at her husband and son then turned and engaged Karasev in pleasant conversation as she led him back through the farm yard and towards the izba.

Once they had become obscured, Vitaly and Pyotr turned to each other and exchanged worried looks.

"Did you recognise any of those other men?" Pyotr asked his son.

"Only one and I can't recall his name," replied Vitaly.

"Which one?"

"The Bear," replied Vitaly with a wry smile.

"He was a bear, wasn't he! And yes, I thought he looked familiar too," stated Pyotr confidently.

"And the other two?" asked Vitaly.

"No idea," replied his father with concern.

"Yeah, me either," stated Vitaly. "Probably just members of the local Soviet. Karasev might act competent but that doesn't mean he is. They're likely here to keep an eye on proceedings. Maybe Karasev can't be trusted?"

"Possibly. Let's get these horses away and join your mother inside."

"Sure thing, Papa," replied Vitaly and they quickly unharnessed and stabled the horses, put away the plough and secured both the barn, with Lex inside, and the paddock gates behind them before heading inside.

As they rounded their izba, they found an automobile parked out in front with a solitary driver seated inside. It was a 1921 Fiat 500 and they couldn't help but be impressed by it. The driver, realising this, gave them a nod and a reluctant wave of his finger before touching the bill of his cap to them.

They turned to each other and shared an appreciative nod at the vehicle's beauty before ascending the stairs, Pyotr leading the way.

Negotiations

The Borisov men entered the izba to find their guests seated together on one side of their dining table while Lena sat alone on the other. She had offered them coffee and cake which all four had accepted graciously and were now devouring when they looked up to find Pyotr and Vitaly entering.

"Comrades, please, join us," said Karasev pleasantly just as Vitaly had shut the door behind them. He motioned for them to join them at the table next to Lena, who looked up at her husband and son nervously. Vitaly and Pyotr both resented being invited to sit down at their own kitchen table but said nothing, instead they turned away from their guests and slowly removed their hats and hung them on the rack inside the door.

Turning back to their guests, they both forced smiles before walking over and taking a seat either side of Lena. Pyotr rested his elbows on the table and intertwined his fingers in front of him while Vitaly rested his in his lap and out of sight beneath the wooden tabletop.

"Allow me to introduce my comrades," stated Karasev,

smiling. "This is comrade Denisov," he indicated to the man on his left, who remained unsmiling. "Comrade Vorshenko," he indicated to the man on his right, who also remained unsmiling, "and comrade Anya," he indicated to the Bear who sat in the seat closest to their large oven and appeared not to have heard him.

"Mrs Borisov was just sharing with me her recollections of her time teaching the children of Virubol," stated Karasev, "and I must say, a most interesting tale it was," he added, looking from Pyotr to Vitaly with an unnerving smile.

"Oh, yes?" replied Pyotr coyly, "and what stories did you tell comrade Karasev?" he asked his wife politely, meeting her eye and smiling.

"Just how Bo... I'm sorry, I mean comrade Karasev, and how mischievous he was as a child," replied Lena apprehensively, catching herself as she did and flashing Karasev an apologetic smile. He nodded curtly in reply.

Vitaly noticed how Karasev, Denisov and Vorshenko moved their eyes from person to person as they spoke. The other man, the Bear, seemed almost disinterested and was picking at the leftover cake crumbs on his plate and observing their stove with apparent interest.

"I was, I admit, often in trouble," he chuckled. "Remember Vitaly?" he asked with a smirk as he locked eyes with his former schoolmate.

"Oh, I remember," replied Vitaly curtly.

"And what do you remember exactly?" asked Karasev, his grin widening. "Specifically, I mean?" he added, nodding his head encouragingly.

"Do you remember the time I beat the shit out of Konstantin Karlov after he hit you with that pine branch?" replied Vitaly nostalgically. He was unsurprised to find himself smiling at the recollection. Meanwhile, Karasev's eyes flashed and his grin faded immediately, replaced instead with a look of disgust.

"Yes, I remember," he replied in somewhat of a low hiss as he ignored Denisov and Vorshenko's quizzical looks sideways at him. "I recall Comrade Karlov being somewhat of a bully during our childhoods. Maybe not so much to you, but certainly to me," he added bitterly. "I therefore doubt you would understand how disappointed I was with how much he has changed," he finished with a sneer.

"Changed?" asked Vitaly as Karasev continued to stare. Vitaly could see the coldness in his eyes but there was a substance there too. Was it bitterness? Hatred? Or desire for revenge?

"Yes, changed, Vitaly," spat Karasev. "I had the pleasure of reacquainting myself with him just last week in Virubol at the Karlov family mill. I just wish the circumstances had been more positive," he stated mockingly. "We, that is my comrades and I," he waved his arms to indicate the men seated next to him, "had the undesirable task of requisitioning their mill for the local Soviet," he finished triumphantly.

So, it was revenge Karasev was after, Vitaly realised, having narrowed it down after his last statement. Is that why he was here? Vitaly searched his mind. When had he wronged Boris Karasev?

Karasev broke eye contact to look at his comrades, who returned malicious grins and nods of approval. Meanwhile, the Bear was now looking out through an open window and had begun to look bored.

"Yes, it was a pleasure to reacquaint ourselves," repeated Karasev with nauseating satisfaction as he slowly turned back to look at Vitaly. "In fact, it's been a pleasure to reacquaint myself with, what would you say, Comrade Denisov? Almost the entire village?"

"Almost," grunted Denisov in reply. He displayed his own sickening smile as he joined Karasev in staring down Vitaly.

"And now, Comrades Borisov and Mrs Borisov, it's a pleasure to reacquaint myself with you here today," said Karasev, looking from one to the other and clapping his hands together with exuberance.

"Is that what this is about?" asked Pyotr sharply. "Some sort of revenge?" And Karasev and his comrades' eyes flicked to Pyotr. Meanwhile, in response to his father's comment, Vitaly felt a sudden rush of respect and appreciation towards him and was overcome with the sudden realisation of just how much they were alike.

"I am in the employ of the local Soviet, comrade," Karasev replied defensively, "and I am simply following orders," he added with another sneer.

"Tell me, comrade, how are the Karlovs?" asked Pyotr, putting emphasis on the word *comrade*.

Karasev's eyes flashed again. "They are well, Comrade Borisov," he replied firmly. "Did you not think they would be?" His eyes bored into Pyotr's before he offered a stumbling reply.

"I uh, no, I wasn't sure. We've not seen them for such a long time you see," replied Pyotr with sudden nervousness. There followed what felt like an eternity of silence while Karasev and his silent comrades continued to stare daggers at him. They'd clearly understood the implication.

"We simply made them an offer," simpered Karasev in mock reassurance, breaking the silence. "The very same offer we have made you and your family which you received in written form several days ago," stated Karasev, and he looked suspiciously from Vitaly to Lena to Pyotr and back again and was unsurprised to find confused expressions upon their faces. "We also received confirmation upon delivery of this written offer so you cannot deny having received it," he added accusatorily.

Both Pyotr and Vitaly looked coldly at Karasev from across the table before Pyotr replied bitterly. "Yes, we received it," he confirmed with a defeated sigh.

"Very good," replied Karasev jovially. "And did you read it, Comrade Borisov?"

"My wife opened it and read it," replied Pyotr.

Their eyes flicked to Lena, who dropped several shades of colour before turning white under their gaze.

"You can confirm this, Mrs Borisov?" asked Karasev, attempting to sound friendly and forcing a smile at the obviously frightened woman.

"Yes, I did, Comrade Karasev," came her reply with surprising confidence and she reciprocated with a forced smile of her own.

"Very good then, very good indeed," replied Karasev happily and he clapped his hands together again. "And did you relay the details of the letter to your husband and son, Mrs Borisov?"

Lena looked sideways at her husband nervously then back towards Karasev, Denisov and Vorshenko, but was careful to avoid their eyes.

"Mrs Borisov?" Karasev asked again, this time more firmly. He had raised his voice and quickly dropped the masquerade of being friendly.

"She tried," interjected Pyotr defiantly as Karasev and his comrades' gazes immediately switched to him and displayed a malevolent curiosity.

"What do you mean, tried?" hissed Karasev.

"I mean that once she told me who it was from, I screwed it up and tossed it into the fire," replied Pyotr with pleasure, and he pointed towards their stove.

Vitaly remained impressed with his father's boldness but knew that, before long, this conversation was likely going to head south. He gauged their guests' reactions, finishing with a glance at the Bear. He was looking away from them so his face was concealed but Vitaly could swear, in the very corner of his mouth was the end of the curl of an appreciative grin.

"A foolish decision, Comrade Borisov," hissed Karasov with displeasure. "Not that it matters I suppose," he added, demeanour changing and breaking into a satisfied grin. "I imagine you already know our offer?"

"Which is?" asked Pyotr boldly, holding the men's attention.

"That your farm, including all buildings, livestock, crops and any other equipment and produce will come under the control of the local Soviet," replied Karasev almost robotically. "And in exchange, your family will be permitted to continue living here with the understanding that you are to operate the farm to our specifications."

Vitaly wondered how many times Karasev had recited this statement.

"Under this agreement you will be provided with any and all additional workers necessary to help with the sowing, harvesting and/or any other farm work. We will also provide the materials, tools and manpower to construct the necessary accommodation to house any additional workers," finished Karasev.

"And if we don't sign?" asked Vitaly defiantly, drawing the men's eyes. His statement had finally attracted the attention of the Bear, who now joined his three comrades as they stared at him.

"That would be most foolish, Comrade Borisov," replied Karasev, who now smiled smugly. "Besides, why would you desire to turn down such a generous offer?"

"Generous!" remarked Pyotr, voice rising to the nervous glances of his wife and son. Their guests' attention now turned back to him while Vitaly could all but shake his head in resignation. Here we go, he thought.

"Yes, generous," replied Karasev sharply, eyes again flashing dangerously, "and I suggest you accept our most generous offer, Comrade Borisov," he added impatiently. "For it is the final offer!"

Vitaly could sense the sudden burst of electricity in the room as all eyes fell on Pyotr expectantly. He looked at his father but was distracted by his mother. She remained chalk white and looked as if she might faint. He quickly put his arm around her in an offer of support. Meanwhile, this was going exactly as he had suspected it would.

"It was my understanding that requisitions were over," stated Pyotr calmly. "Was it not Lenin after all who instituted the New Economic Policy, effectively ending war communism?" he asked. "A policy which has been in place for some months now," he finished.

"It was comrade Lenin, and now me, my comrades and the leader and other members of the local Soviet reinstating requisitions in response to the recent famine caused by the ongoing war with the whites," retorted Karasev sharply.

"But the war is over!" spat Vitaly angrily before Karasev turned to look at him.

"An irrelevant point, comrade," replied Karasev coldly. "My offer is non-negotiable!" He smiled maliciously.

"And what if, hypothetically, I said fuck your deal?" asked Pyotr with more boldness and defiance than before.

There it was! If Vitaly was being honest, he couldn't help but be impressed with his father's audacity and brevity at a moment like this. The man was bold, although judging by the look on Karasev's face he didn't agree. His current expression indicated he was ready to explode at the insult his father had offered. Impressively, when Karasev finally responded, his voice was soft and calm.

"Fuck my deal, you say," replied Karasev coolly. "Fuck my deal?" he repeated, his voice rising this time. "That, Comrade Borisov, is the wrong answer!" And by now he looked quite menacing.

"Yes, I thought so," replied Pyotr, his temper rising. "In fact, I'll go one better. Fuck you *and* your deal!" he said to Karasev, pointing at him. "And, fuck you, and you, and you too," he added, pointing in turn to each man sitting across the table from him. Besides the Bear, who Vitaly was sure was finding this whole conversation amusing, the other men scowled and fidgeted in their seats uncomfortably while glowering at Pyotr.

Well, there goes the farm, Papa, Vitaly thought, as he watching anxiously for the men's reactions. This could get ugly.

Vitaly couldn't help but be impressed with Karasev's self-control. He remained calm before replying again softly, "You do of course have two other options here, Pyotr. Sadly however, both of them result in you losing your farm," he stated coldly before his face broke into a malicious grin. "Option one, which is my personal favourite, is arrest followed by a lengthy prison sentence. Option two is exile," he added, now smiling gleefully.

"Which one did the Karlovs choose?" spat Pyotr, who had by now completely abandoned inhibition. Vitaly looked from his father to his mother to Karasev and back. His mother was getting paler by the minute so he gave her shoulders a gentle squeeze and she rested her head on his shoulder.

"Is she okay?" came a deep voice from across the table. It was the Bear. With surprise, Vitaly looked again at his mother then back to the Bear and then Karasev.

"Mama?" asked Vitaly softly. "Are you okay?"

Turning her head towards him, she smiled at him before replying. "Hmm. Not to worry, Vitaly, I'm just feeling a little lightheaded. I suspect it's from the heat," she finished weakly as their guests watched her suspiciously. The only one who looked concerned was the Bear, Vitaly noticed.

She turned to look at her guests. "Would you care for some more coffee, Comrade Karasev? And how about you comrades?" She looked at them all in turn. Karasev and his men looked back bemused then shook their heads.

"I'll get some more," she stated, ignoring their replies before rising from her chair.

"No, no, it is okay, Mrs Borisov," came Karasev's high voice. But this too was ignored.

"Mama, no, it's okay," pleaded Vitaly, who grabbed at her elbow as Pyotr watched on with concern. Alas, she pushed her chair back and took several shaky steps before she stopped and suddenly crumpled to the floor.

"Mama!" Vitaly yelled, jumping out of his seat. He raced to her side and fell to his knees on the floor. Instantaneously, pain shot through his right leg but he ignored it, choosing instead to focus on his mother.

"Lena!" came Pyotr's voice before he too joined his son's side.

There were the sounds of hurried footsteps and scraping chairs on timber as the room filled with activity. Vitaly was surprised to be met at his mother's side by the Bear, this Comrade Anya, and he nodded to him appreciatively. Meanwhile Karasev and the other two men had risen but not to offer their support.

"Come, Anya," barked Karasev to his comrade. "This meeting is over. Leave them be. They will handle her," he added unsympathetically.

"Comrade Karasev, we cannot just leave in a situation like this," barked back Comrade Anya. He lifted Lena's head up and placed a balled-up blanket under her head that Pyotr had handed him.

"We have seen these theatrics before," replied Karasev. "I'm sure once we leave, she'll be perfectly fine," he added sarcastically, rolling his eyes at his two comrades who stood next to him and chuckled appreciatively in response. "It is pathetic," he spat before turning and heading for the izba's door.

Vitaly was incensed by Karasev's disregard for his mother's wellbeing. He'd only ever seen her faint once and knew instinctively that this was no act. He looked at his father and at the Bear, who was now patting the top of his mother's hand soothingly. Her eye lids flickered then opened, and suddenly, she was staring up at the three men through a mask of confusion.

"What happened?" she asked in a whisper.

"You fainted, Mrs Borisov," came the Bear's reply and smiled kindly down at her. Pyotr and Vitaly both nodded their heads in agreement as she turned and looked from one to the other.

"Oh, I'm so sorry," she said with embarrassment.

"Don't be silly," replied the Bear, smiling again. "Now, I'm confident you'll be okay but do you think you can sit up?"

"Come, Anya! We are leaving here," came Karasev's increasingly angry voice, and it became obvious to Vitaly that Karasev didn't like being ignored. "Comrade Borisov, Vitaly and Mrs Borisov, you have exhausted my very limited patience. I regret to inform you that I will be returning here tomorrow with the Militsiya and placing you under arrest. Say goodbye to your farm," he finished coldly.

Vitaly had heard enough. He looked at his mother then his

father and finally at the Bear. Their eyes lingered and the Bear silently shook his head in warning at what Vitaly was thinking. Ignoring this, he stood up quickly, turned and walked briskly towards Karasev, who was now discussing something with his comrades. As Vitaly approached, he clenched his fist tightly and swung back his arm then yelled, "Hey, Boris? Fuck you!" before he unleashed on his unsuspecting target.

"Vitaly!" screamed his father, but his voice was drowned out by the sickening crunch Vitaly's clenched fist made when it met Karasev's face. It was a good hit, landing squarely in the middle of his head, shattering jaw, splattering nose and dislodging several teeth which bounced as they hit the wooden floor.

Karasev emitted a deep grunt as he went stumbling backwards into the izba's wall before coming to a stop face down on the floor. All Denisov and Vorshenko could do was stare at Vitaly in disbelief. Finally, they both dropped to their knees to check on their injured comrade who had begun emitting a very unpleasant sound. One similar to a wounded animal.

Vitaly stood there inhaling and exhaling deeply as the adrenalin coursed through his veins. He looked down at his hand and realised the punch must have been well placed. He clenched and unclenched his fist expecting pain that didn't come. Upon closer inspection, all he noticed was a slight red discoloration across his knuckles and he flexed them again uncertainly just to make sure they were okay. Everything felt fine.

He looked down at Karasev and his blood quickly came back up to a boil. Suddenly he was back in the army and this was combat on the Eastern Front. He looked at his rifle hanging from the rack behind the door and stepped over and grabbed it down. He quickly removed several rounds of ammunition from his bandolier and loaded them before racking in a round. Now he was ready and he raised the weapon and pointed it at Karasev and the men crouching by his side.

"Hey, Boches!" he yelled instinctively, completely unaware he'd just used the Russian term for Germans during the war. Getting their attention nevertheless; they raised their hands and looked at him fearfully. "Get that piece of shit up and get the fuck out of my izba!" he yelled angrily and they grabbed Karasev under the arms and awkwardly lifted him up into a standing position.

Despite the intensity of the situation, Vitaly was shocked and nauseated when he saw the state of Karasev's face. He was instantly disgusted with himself for the damage he had caused. He'd completely mutilated him with one punch. Blood dripped from Karasev's open mouth and broken nose and his right eye had already swelled shut. All the while he continued to make that horrible noise and appeared to be struggling for breath.

"You'll pay for this, comrade," threatened Denisov, and he looked at Vitaly with reciprocal disgust. "You and your entire family," he added, indicating Pyotr and Lena with a nod of his head. Both his parents had by now risen from the floor and his mother had been returned to her seat with assistance from the Bear. They all watched on fearfully.

"Yeah? Fuck you!" yelled Vitaly. He was struggling to wrest control of his emotions despite knowing it was in his best interest to do so. He was angry but he also felt guilty. Had Karasev deserved that? The little voice in his head said yes, but another voice said no. "Fuck off!" he yelled, this time to himself but the command was interpreted as being for those present.

"Let us pass then, Borisov," said a rattled Vorshenko as he

strained from the effort of holding up the dead weight that was Karasev.

"Vitaly?" came his father's voice from his right. He turned to look at him whilst keeping the gun levelled on their guests. "Let them pass," he pleaded as Karasev emitted a gurgling sound. "He's in, by the looks of it, pretty serious need of medical attention," he added firmly, nodding his head at his son.

"Okay, okay," replied Vitaly calmly. Keeping his rifle raised threateningly, he turned and opened the door before taking several steps backwards. With hesitation, Denisov and Vorshenko dragged the lifeless form of Karasev out through the door. At the top of the stairs Denisov handed Karasev off to Vorshenko before turning back to speak to the Bear.

"Are you coming, Anya?" he asked his comrade loudly whilst eyeballing Vitaly cautiously.

"Yes, comrade Denisov," he replied calmly before Denisov quickly turned and descended the stairs. He could be heard yelling outside to Vorshenko and at the driver whose name turned out to be Rivov.

The Bear took his time though and courteously thanked Lena for the coffee and cake before patting her on the shoulder gently and shaking Pyotr's hand. He looked apprehensively at Vitaly and began slowly walking across the room before he stopped where Karasev had gone down and removed a kerchief from his pocket.

"He might want these," he said, smiling reassuringly at Vitaly. He bent down and started collecting the loose teeth now scattered about and carefully placed them in the kerchief, "and you don't need to point that at me," he stated calmly to Vitaly.

"If it's all the same to you, I'd prefer not to take any chances," came Vitaly's reply.

"Well, that's understandable," replied the Bear with a snort. "Some advice though, Vitaly," he offered. "While I mean you no harm, the men outside do and retribution will be quick." He tied the teeth securely in the kerchief and stuffed it into his pants pocket. Vitaly couldn't explain it, but he felt a profound sense of calmness in the Bear's presence. Indicating this, he offered the Bear an appreciative nod before he slowly and tentatively lowered his rifle.

"I thank you for attending to my mother," stated Vitaly calmly before he looked at her and smiled.

"My pleasure." The Bear nodded. "Now take my advice," he continued, "and run."

"Run? Run where?"

"Into the woods. Take only what you need including your rifle there and that pistol," he stated, and he pointed towards the rack behind the door that Vitaly's holster dangled from. Secured inside was his army issued pistol.

"Yes, Vitaly," interrupted Pyotr. "Go through the woods to your uncle's in Kyrubol," he added.

"Even better," came the Bear's reply and he looked at Pyotr and smiled appreciatively. "I'm sure he would be happy for a visit from his nephew," he added.

"But I can't stay there!" replied Vitaly, waving his arms and rifle around in protest.

"Why not?" asked the Bear.

"Because I can't!" Vitaly replied pleadingly.

"Vitaly, I've told you before, Anatoly too, you're no more responsible for Evgeny's death than I am!" remarked Pyotr to his son. Vitaly looked at his father then his mother and back to the Bear, who now looked puzzled at this change in conversation.

Shaking his head, the Bear said, "Listen, Vitaly, just go. Wait for me and my comrades to leave and go."

"But what about them?" Vitaly enquired, indicating his parents.

"They will be fine," replied the Bear confidently as Vitaly searched his face. His calming presence continuing to have an effect.

"Listen to Comrade Anya, Vitaly," begged his father. "Your mother and I will be okay. We will agree to their deal, if necessary," he finished, with Lena silently nodding her approval from her seat at the kitchen table.

Vitaly locked eyes with his father again then moved onto his mother before resigning himself to his fate. "Okay, but you best be on your way then, Anya," he stated calmly to the Bear. "They're getting inpatient out there. I can still hear them yelling."

"It will not be a pleasant ride back into Virubol I suspect," replied the Bear with resignation. "But I will bid you good day and impress upon you not to worry. I assure you your parents will be okay."

Vitaly flashed an uncertain yet appreciative smile at the Bear, who reciprocated in kind before he turned and exited the izba and closed the door behind him. The Borisov's remained behind in silence and listened to Anya's heavy footsteps as he descended the stairs. Suddenly, the Fiat's engine became engaged, which instantly drowned out the yelling coming from its passengers. After a few loud revs the tyres skidded on the gravel road and the noise of the engine began to slowly fade away.

FLIGHT

"I'll grab you some bread and cheese. Fill your canteen and take a spare just in case," said his mother anxiously, having risen from the chair and begun racing around the izba frantically.

"Mama, calm down," came Vitaly's concerned reply.

"Yes, Lena, please listen to your son," came Pyotr's plea but it was to no avail. He stepped towards her and embraced her tightly by wrapping his arms around her body and locking her elbows to her side before whispering in her ear.

Vitaly watched on as he sat his rifle down beside the door before walking across the room and into his corner. He grabbed his bag and stuffed a spare shirt and trousers inside along with his tobacco pouch and cigarettes. He opened his bureau drawer and withdrew his flask and took a quick swig before tossing that inside too.

He stopped and splashed some water on his face, which felt colder than before. He looked up and observed himself in the mirror again and was startled to discover how red his face was. Was it sunburn? No, it was the after effects of how worked up he had been only moments before.

He turned around to find his parents in a warm embrace and his mother sobbing quietly into his father's shoulder. He felt a pang of guilt at the sight. He had caused this, he thought to himself, and now he was going to run away. He walked towards his parents, dropped his bag and then threw his arms around them both. His mother buried her tear-streaked face in Vitaly's chest and wrapped her arms around his waist. Pyotr disengaged and stepped back to observe the sad sight.

"Come, Lena," came Pyotr's voice as he reached out and placed his hand on her shoulder supportively.

"Mama?" asked Vitaly, looking down at her. "I must go," he added.

"I know," she replied resignedly, looking him in the eye and sniffling. "I've got you some cheese and bread. It's tied inside those kerchiefs on the table," she finished.

"Thank you, Mama," he replied gratefully before leaning down and kissing her gently on her forehead. She looked up at him and smiled but still wouldn't let him go.

"Lena!" said Pyotr with urgency. "Let him go or they'll be back before you know it!"

"Let go, Mama," pleaded Vitaly, nodding his head in agreement as mother and son looked into each other's eyes. "Please," he added, urgency and anxiety rising in his voice at his father's reminder.

"I'm sorry, Vitaly," said Lena, shaking her head. Reluctantly, she finally let him go. Her hands now free, she wiped away a tear running down her cheek.

"It's okay, Mama," replied Vitaly with an affectionate smile. He reached over and took the cheese and bread she had wrapped for him before picking up his bag and placing them inside. "Have you a spare canteen, Papa?" he asked his father, turning to him.

"Yes, Vitaly," he replied and he waved the hand that held it. "It needs filling but we can do that at the well. You should go. I will see you out," he finished with an uncertain smile.

"Okay, Papa," replied Vitaly before turning to his mother. "I love you, Mama. Take care," he said before kissing her on the cheek. He turned away abruptly afterwards lest he be caught again in her vicelike embrace.

"I love you too," came her soft reply as tears began to fall in earnest from her eyes.

Pyotr led the way, opening the door and looking back to his son. He watched as Vitaly collected his rifle and pistol then some spare ammunition which joined the other belongings inside his bag. He put on his cap and nodded at his father, which confirmed he was ready to depart so he slung his bag over his shoulder and the two men stepped through the door before Pyotr closed it behind them.

They descended the stairs in silence then turned and entered the yard and crossed it briskly in the direction of the well. "Papa," Vitaly said, gaining his father's attention. "I must grab something," he explained before he quickly disappeared in the direction of their barn before returning holding another flask filled with vodka.

Vitaly held it up to show his father and gave a wry smile, much to his father's disapproval. They continued on towards the well where his father cranked the pulley and carefully filled the empty canteen until it was filled to the brim. Vitaly watched on, both men speaking little in the interim.

Securing the stopper, Pyotr handed his son the canteen before they turned and headed towards the back gate and the fields beyond. They arrived at the gate and turned to each other, shaking hands and embracing warmly.

"Take care, son," said Pyotr affectionately.

"You too, Papa," replied Vitaly, smiling. There was an awkward silence that followed as neither man knew what to say to the other in the circumstances.

"Say hello to Anatoly for me," requested Pyotr jovially, relieved at finally having something to say.

"I will." Vitaly nodded assuredly before he opened the gate and walked through. He turned back and pushed it closed behind him before Pyotr grabbed one of the railings in his hands and shook it, ensuring it was shut tight.

"Don't forget Lex is locked inside the barn, Papa," said Vitaly.

"I won't," replied Pyotr. "Actually, do you want to take him with you?"

"No thank you, Papa," replied Vitaly politely. "I will be in a hurry and you know how he likes to chase everything," he added, smiling at the recollection.

"Yes, he does," replied Pyotr with a chuckle. "I'll wait until you've disappeared into the wood before I let him out, otherwise he might follow you," he finished.

"Good idea, Papa." Vitaly smiled and with one final look and nod, turned away from his father and looked towards the woods beyond their fields and began what would be a very long walk.

His heart and mind were wracked with worry as he crossed the field. Was he doing the right thing? he thought to himself. One thing he did know for certain was he wouldn't be looking back because he knew his father would be watching him and remain doing so until he disappeared into the woods. He hoped his parents were going to be okay. The bear at least appeared certain of their safety. Perhaps he knew something Vitaly and his parents didn't?

He reached the tree line, which also indicated the

boundary of their property, and was grateful for the shade the trees provided as he crossed over it. It was still early, perhaps eleven a.m., but warm and he had many miles to cover. He was optimistic though; he had made the walk many times before the war but zero times since. It used to take him around three and a half hours including a couple of rest and drink stops and that was walking at a brisk pace. Therefore, this would be the biggest test he had put his knee to and it already ached. It almost always ached.

He followed a rough path that he himself had helped carve over the years. His grandfather had been the first to use it followed by his own father and uncle Anatoly. Then came himself and his cousins Evgeny and Sofia who would spend nights camped out here in the wilderness. He loved the woods. The smell of the pine, spruce, larch and fir trees was almost therapeutic to him.

He reminisced as he walked. He stepped around and then under a large felled pine that he and his cousins had played on years before and was reminded of Evgeny, his poor dead cousin, taken too young. Would Anatoly be happy to see him? Would he welcome him into his home? He worried, as he always did, that Anatoly would hold him responsible for Evgeny's demise. He also knew that that fear was irrational; Anatoly had gladly embraced him the first time he had seen him after he returned from the war.

Then there was Aunt Irina. She was a sweet woman, tough, yes, but sweet. Together, Anatoly and Irina had operated the neighbouring farm to Vitaly and his parents back when the children had been young. But that was before they sold up and moved to Kyrubol. There they had purchased another larger one that backed onto the northern end of these very woods, making them essentially neighbours but with twelve miles between their back gates.

As he walked, he crossed several small streams, passed through the occasional clearing and walked up and down numerous small inclines. The woods were thick and relatively untouched and full of wildlife. He recalled a story his grandfather had told him and his cousins when they were children which explained why they were in such pristine condition and why so few people ventured inside.

The story of Baba Yaga, as his grandfather had told it, had fascinated Vitaly as a child. His grandfather had described her as a hideous old woman who would always carry a mortar and pestle with which she would grind up unruly and misbehaving children. She had lived in a house that spun on chicken legs and she may have had three sisters who all went by the same name.

She could also appear as a young and beautiful sorceress, depending on the circumstances, who would help a lost traveller by offering wisdom and magical reward. This was the lasting image Vitaly had in mind from his childhood. He had longed to meet her in hopes of marrying her and developing his own magical abilities and he found himself smiling to himself at the recollection.

Evgeny however had been afraid of Baba Yaga and been reluctant to venture into the wood in fear of her. One day though, through a combination of teasing and coercion, Vitaly had managed to lure his then young cousin into the wood on an adventure. He had dressed Sofia up to frighten Evgeny and succeeded. Evgeny had gone screaming out of the wood and run to his father who was in the fields sowing at the time with Pyotr and his grandfather.

After their parents' scolding, their grandfather had taken the three children aside and explained that Baba Yaga wouldn't hurt them because he had made a deal with her. As long as the children were well behaved and treated the forest and all that dwell within the trees, the river and streams with kindness and respect, they would be not only safe to venture inside but protected by Baba Yaga's magic.

That lie had done the trick and from then on, the three children, occasionally accompanied by their parents and more often by their grandfather, would venture inside and spend endless hours at play. They envisaged imaginary kingdoms and fought invisible enemies in grand battles like those of years gone by. "For Russia!" they would yell. They elected their grandfather as Czar of this realm and swore fealty and allegiance to him as his loyal subjects.

Lost in his memories, Vitaly had lost track of time and distance but suddenly found himself in a familiar location. It was where he estimated to be the halfway mark of the journey between his father's and uncle's farms so he stopped to open his canteen before drinking thirstily. To his pleasant surprise, his knee and leg appeared to be holding up surprisingly well despite still aching.

He dropped his rifle and bag down onto the ground and opened the latter to withdraw his flask. He placed it on the ground and replaced the canteen's lid before dropping it into the bag in the flask's place. He again picked up his flask and stood up before taking a very satisfying swig of delicious vodka and letting out a sigh of relief.

He picked up his bag and rifle and sat himself down amongst the jumbled roots under his favourite fir tree and made himself comfortable. He took another swig of the vodka before opening his bag again and withdrawing his bread and cheese. He ate hungrily, depleted from his journey so far. He'd made good time, distracted by his thoughts and memories.

It would be early afternoon now, he guessed, looking to the sky and observing the shadows made by the trees surrounding him. He sat quietly and listened to the sounds of the nearby stream as it flowed quickly by. This stream was unusual in that it appeared to never dry up regardless of how hot and dry the summers became and he was grateful for that, for it was a great source of drinking water. His guess was that it was spring fed and would flow into the nearby river.

Several more minutes passed as he sat there. He could hear birds above him singing to one another over the crunching of his jaw as he ate. He rubbed his knee cap absentmindedly before taking another swig of vodka. That had better do it, he thought, otherwise I won't make it to uncle Anatoly's. So, he rewrapped what remained of his bread and cheese and replaced the lid on his vodka and returned all three to the confines of his bag. He changed his mind about the vodka and removed it again and dropped it into his pants pocket.

His body cracked as he stood up and stretched out. He lifted his bag back onto his shoulder and swung his rifle over the other and set off again on his journey. The second half would be much the same as the first; he would transverse similar terrain and remain enclosed within the dense woods.

The West Siberian Plain was a vast lowland of diverse environments and ecosystems. To the west rose the Urals mountains, to the east flowed the Yenisei River and to the southeast stood the Altai Mountains. Generally, the area was poorly drained and consisted of vast swamps and floodplains. The land around and between Virubol and Kyrubol was one of the exceptions. It was well drained and sat higher than its surroundings and was a mixture of rich woodlands and farmlands ideal for wheat and other crop production. Winters were cold and harsh but the people managed to survive.

His thoughts drifted back to his parents' predicament and he wondered how soon it would be before the local Soviet returned, this time accompanied by the militsiya. It would be him they were after, but what would they do when they discovered his absence? Would they arrest his parents or would their acquiescence to their demands be enough to spare them incarceration? He remained hopeful.

His thoughts then drifted to Boris Karasev and what kind of condition he was in. Upon further reflection, Vitaly found that he didn't regret hitting him. He did however regret and feel guilt at the level of damage he had quite obviously caused his former childhood playmate. Had Karasev changed? Or had he always been that way?

Perhaps he had merely been unable to manoeuvre himself into a position from which he could exercise power over others and reveal his true self and nature. It was Bolshevism that had given him the opportunity. In the absence of the ruling class, who Vitaly readily admitted were not necessarily good at leadership, people who shouldn't wield power had been given it and those that weren't were often victimised.

Lenin and his followers had preached equality through revolution and Vitaly himself had fallen under that spell. It was easy to, really. As he lay there in hospital at the Winter Palace in Petrograd, convalescing for months from his injuries, he frequently spoke to fellow soldiers who sought out their fellow comrades who had given their service most devastatingly in the name of the Czar.

In his boredom and despite visits from the Czarina and her admittedly charming and beautiful daughters, he had agreed to join the Bolsheviks upon discharge. This would be his chance, he had thought, to escape the farm and his rural peasant life that awaited him upon his return to Virubol after the war.

He had still been in the hospital during the February revolution which saw the overthrow of the Czar and Alexander Kerensky take control of the new provisional government. He appeared the ideal man to lead post-Imperial Russia as he bridged the gap between the Duma and Bolsheviks.

But he had made mistakes and costly ones at that. Firstly, his decision under pressure from Russia's allies, the British, French and later the Americans to continue the war against the Germans was unpopular and led to mass mutinies amongst Russian soldiers who had then travelled to Petrograd and joined with the Bolsheviks.

Secondly, in response to the Kornilov affair, an attempted coup by the Russian Army commander in chief, Lavr Kornilov, Kerensky had rearmed the Bolsheviks in Petrograd. They would then turn on Kerensky the following October in another revolution and from this point on, Lenin would rule over Russia.

Yes, the last decade had brought many changes to Russia, thought Vitaly. He was only twenty-four and in his life time Russia had undergone a very rapid industrialisation, three wars, three revolutions, numerous assassinations, one abdication and the ending of a three-hundred-year-old dynasty. And what was next? He couldn't guess but hoped, however reluctantly, to be around to see it.

With that thought, he came to the edge of the wood and could see in the distance the open paddock of his uncle's farm. Relief and anxiety flooded his consciousness. He begrudged having to explain the purpose of his visit, although in doing so he knew Uncle Anatoly and Aunt Irina would understand. Or at least, he hoped they would.

Stepping out from under the shade of the trees, he exited the dense wood into the hot afternoon sun which blazed angrily down upon him. Using the back of his sleeve, he wiped away the perspiration that had formed under the brim of his cap and now ran down his forehead and face.

He looked up at the hazy blue horizon as he entered the

neatly ploughed field and lowered his eyes to look into the distance at his uncle's izba. It was similar in appearance, as most were in this area, to his own family. He would hazard a guess and say they were perhaps slightly better off than his parents but the difference was negligible and was of no importance to either family.

They were and remained on good terms. Uncle Anatoly and his father were their parents only children, Anatoly being the younger by two years. They had grown up close after losing their mother as children and were raised primarily by their father with the assistance of his mother and aunt.

He reached the yard gate and climbed over it, landing with a thud on the cobbled stones on the other side. The yard was extremely neat, with everything packed away. Their three horses lazed inside their pens inside the barn along with their two dairy cows, who inspected Vitaly with curiosity as he passed by.

His footsteps reverberated around the yard as he headed for the izba's side door, a luxury his own family didn't possess but would allow more heat to escape from inside during the winter time. He stopped at the bottom of the wooden steps and took one last look around the yard, inspecting it for signs of human activity, but couldn't see or hear anybody. He shrugged to himself and ascended the stairs. Upon reaching the top step, he could hear the voice of his uncle inside.

He waited a moment before knocking, indecision clouding his mind. Had it been a bad decision to come here? Would his presence here cause the local Soviet to pursue Anatoly and his family like they had threatened to do to his? Perhaps he should just turn around and disappear back into the woods and wait a few days before reemerging.

He could survive. His grandfather had taught him and Evgeny how to hunt and survive in the wilderness, at least for a short time. The woods were filled with all kinds of game, and his diet could be diverse and even exotic if he wanted. He had his rifle and ample ammunition, so why not? His mind raced. He knew he was being foolish and that would be unnecessary. If he was ever guilty of anything, it was of overthinking, so with a deep breath and steely determination, he reached up and knocked on his uncle's door.

Kyrubol

His uncle's voice stopped and for a moment there was nothing but silence from behind the izba's door. The scraping of chairs legs and footsteps on the wooden floor indicated that someone was coming to answer it. It swung open and there stood his Uncle Anatoly.

"Vitaly," he said, confused. "Vitaly!" he repeated, but this time with the full weight of the surprise he felt. He stepped forward and threw his arms around his nephew and embraced him warmly. Vitaly looked into the izba over his uncle's shoulder and was met by looks of surprise from both his aunt Irina and cousin Sofia before they broke into smiles.

Anatoly released his nephew and stood back before taking his face in his hands.

"It's good to see you, son," he exclaimed, beaming.

"Hello uncle," replied Vitaly, smiling before Anatoly let go of his face and pulled him in for another embrace.

Irina and Sofia had reached him now and stood directly behind Anatoly just inside the doorway.

"What brings you to Kyrubol, Vitaly?" asked his aunt with interest.

Beaming, Anatoly released his nephew again and turned to his wife.

"Look who's here, Irina," he said, putting his arm around Vitaly's shoulders and giving him an affectionate squeeze.

"Well, let him in, Anatoly!" came her amused reply before she too embraced him warmly and planted an affectionate kiss on his cheek. "It's wonderful to see you, Vitaly," she added before pulling away and looking into his eyes.

Sofia stepped forward and looked at her cousin with interest. "I suppose you'll be expecting a cuddle from me too?" she asked with sarcasm.

"I suppose," he mumbled back through a sheepish grin.

"Well, come on then, funny man," she replied breaking into a big smile before they too embraced. "I thought you'd forgotten about me, your favourite cousin," she said directly into his ear before stepping back and looking at him quizzically.

He stood there and was observed with great interest by all three of his relatives. They were happy to see him, it appeared, and for that he was relieved. He felt foolish. Deep down he knew this was how it was going to be. He felt a sudden rush of appreciation and gratitude towards them.

"So, what brings you to Kyrubol, Vitaly?" asked Anatoly.

"Yeah, funny man?" asked Sofia tartly. "It's not exactly on the way to anywhere!" she added rolling her eyes.

"Um, I," he mumbled, unsure of where to begin with his explanation as all three family members looked on suspiciously. His face must've spoken the words he couldn't because their facial expressions changed to reflect their growing concern at his purpose.

"Vitaly? Is everything okay?" asked Aunt Irina softly whilst continuing to look into his eyes. Like his mother, she was someone he found it hard to lie to.

"Well, I, um. It's embarrassing," replied Vitaly with uncertainty.

"Well, out with it, son," interjected Anatoly impatiently and he looked upon his nephew with sternness.

"I'm in trouble," said Vitaly, his voice trembling.

"What trouble?" asked Anatoly and Irina in unison and they turned to each other and exchanged worried looks. Sofia looked on, her facial expression remaining passive and almost unconcerned.

"Trouble with the local Soviet," replied Vitaly, wincing. He had suddenly become aware of how painful his knee felt and reached down and rubbed it. His uncle noticed.

"How about we sit down first and then discuss this trouble," said Anatoly, looking at Vitaly before turning again to his wife and giving her a nod. She reciprocated her understanding and walked over to the stove and adjusted the kettle. Anatoly took Vitaly's bag and rifle and sat them behind the door, which he then closed. Vitaly, somewhat stiffly, shuffled towards the kitchen table.

"Come and sit, son. Are you alright to walk?" asked Anatoly, concerned.

"Yes, I'm fine. Just a little pain. It's been so long since I've walked from Virubol. My knee isn't used to it," Vitaly explained as he took the seat his uncle had pulled out for him.

"Vodka?" asked his uncle.

"Um, no, I best not," replied Vitaly and he pulled out his flask and showed it to him, giving his uncle a sheepish smile.

Irina removed the whistling kettle from the top of the stove and Sofia produced four ceramic mugs and placed them in the middle of the table. All four of them took a seat, Anatoly across from Vitaly, Irina next to her husband and across from Sofia, who now began to pour the boiling coffee.

There were a few minutes of silence, broken only by the sound of silver teaspoons clinking against the side of ceramic mugs after they added their sugar and stirred. Vitaly had become very interested in the contents of his mug as his uncle, aunt and cousin exchanged anxious glances. It was Sofia who broke the silence.

"Do you remember Edgar Tarlov, Vitaly?" she enquired with an interested look.

"Edgar Tarlov?" He replied, confused.

"Yes. Edgar Tarlov," she repeated, now looking serious.

"No, I don't think I do Sofia." He replied. "Should I?"

"He fought alongside you. Or at least that's what he told me," She replied sharply.

"I don't know the name," Stated Vitaly, racking his brain in search of a memory.

"It was during the Brusilov offensive. That's where you were wounded, right?"

"That's correct," replied Vitaly, as he became increasingly uncomfortable with the line of questioning.

She waited in silent anticipation of an elaborated reply that would not come. Realising this, she continued, "Well, anyways, he was a medic during the war. He's the assistant to the doctor that visits our villages and is in training to become one himself. He told me that he was there the day you were wounded and that he saw it happen. According to him, he was the first medic on the scene and helped transfer you to the field hospital."

Her parents looked on with concern as Vitaly continued to stare into his mug. There was a long silence. Plenty of time for Vitaly to think.

"Sofia, you know your cousin is reticent to recall his service in the war," scolded her mother whilst looking nervously at Vitaly. Mother and daughter then exchanged very different expressions. Irina now looked angry; Sofia on the other hand gave her mother a derisive look and shrugged her shoulders carelessly.

"Edgar told me that the best way to deal with your issues is to talk about them," Sofia exclaimed defiantly before moving her gaze back to her cousin.

"I don't remember him okay, Sofia!" snapped Vitaly in frustration, his knee giving a painful throb. Perhaps it was from the recollection of the war? "I passed out when I was wounded, or at least that's what I was told," he added angrily. "The first thing I remember, clearly that is, is being in the Winter Palace in Petrograd. And I would appreciate it if you dropped it!"

Scowling at her cousin, Sofia threw herself into the back of her chair. "Well, that's more than we've ever gotten out of you before!" she said tartly, covering the fact her feelings had been hurt. She was only trying to help.

"Leave it, Sofia," scolded her mother again before she turned to her nephew. "Will you tell us about this trouble with the local Soviet, Vitaly? How can your uncle and I help?" She asked, changing the subject.

"Yes, Vitaly, how can we help?" added Anatoly supportively.

"I'm not sure that you can," came Vitaly's soft reply.

"Tell us what happened and let us decide," said Anatoly.

"And you hush, Sofia!" interjected Irina, holding up her hand and stopping her daughter from interrupting, Sofia scowling at her mother in response.

"Go on Vitaly," encouraged Irina and she smiled pleasantly at him between sips of her coffee. Everyone looked and listened intently as Vitaly spoke.

"Did my father tell you about our expected visit by them?" asked Vitaly.

"Yes," replied Anatoly. "The last time I spoke to him. That was several weeks ago though," he added with a serious expression as Irina nodded her head in agreement.

"Well, that visit was earlier today," replied Vitaly. "We received a letter around the time you spoke, obviously before, but probably only by a few days. It explained that we would be visited by members of the local Soviet regarding the acquisition of the farm."

"Yes, that's what Pyotr told me." Interrupted Anatoly.

"Well, do you remember Boris Karasev?" asked Vitaly.

"Yes," replied his aunt and uncle, again in unison.

"He's in charge," said Vitaly.

"They gave Boris Karasev, that little weed, power?" replied Sofia, stunned.

"Unfortunately." Vitaly smiled, recollecting the similarities in her statement to the one made by his mother that very morning.

Sofia looked confused by his reaction. "Did I say something funny?" she asked very seriously.

"No, Sofia. Well, no and yes. You sounded exactly like Mama just then. Almost to the word," Vitaly explained before hastily reapplying a more serious expression.

"And what happened?" asked Anatoly.

"They arrived this morning and we had a brief discussion about our options," replied Vitaly.

"Which were?" His uncle asked again.

"Live on the farm and run it for the Soviets, or arrest and removal. And you'll love this uncle Anatoly, the third option given was exile."

Anatoly looked at his nephew with raised eyebrows before scowling. "Fucking Soviets!" he said with venom. "They've forced so many decent Russians to flee this country already!" He finished the sentence by banging his fist on the table.

"But what happened, Vitaly?" asked his aunt, who had remained focused on the issue at hand.

"Papa was blunt with Karasev, who didn't like it, and Mama fainted," replied Vitaly.

"Oh, no! Is she okay?" asked Irina and Sofia together.

"She was when I left. That is, she was sitting at the table and her colour had returned," replied Vitaly.

"That's good then," said Irina, smiling warmly. "I wouldn't know her as a fainter. Although, now that you mention it, I do recall it happening one day, years ago, back at our old farm in Virubol."

"Yes, I remember," said Vitaly.

"And what happened after that?" asked Irina.

"Karasev suspected Mama of acting," replied Vitaly.

"No!" interrupted the three in unison, their anger and disgust obvious. Anatoly slammed his fist down on the table again causing Irina to jump.

"Yeah!" said Vitaly. "So, I got up and punched him," he added very seriously before nodded his head.

"Excellent!" His uncle clapped in approval and Sofia laughed with delight. Meanwhile, Irina looked on, neither smiling or clapping; instead, her face was a mask of worry.

"You shouldn't have done that, Vitaly," Irina said in an almost whisper.

"What do you mean, Irina!?" interjected Anatoly and he turned to look at her. His face displayed both surprise and disappointment at her comment.

Irina turned her head and looked at Anatoly. "Why do you think he is here?" she asked her husband whilst he looked back at her with confusion. "He's here because he has had to flee for the safety of himself, Pyotr and Lena," she exclaimed. "You know as well as I do, Anatoly, these people are dangerous and, worse yet, capable," she finished.

"He did the right thing!" Anatoly replied with annoyance.

"The right thing to do, as much as it upsets me to say it, is to say yes, comrade, of course, comrade, what else can I do for you, comrade and so on," Irina replied derisively.

"Irina!" Anatoly said, but he was quickly interrupted by Sofia.

"Mama's right, Papa. Edgar would tell you the same thing."

"Edgar, Edgar, Edgar!" he replied mockingly while waving his arms in the air. "That boy is about as thick as our last Czar," he added spitefully.

"Anatoly!" growled Irina, before, with a hurt look, Sofia replied.

"I knew you didn't like him!" she said with conviction. "He's actually really nice, Papa!"

"Listen you two, stop it!" interjected Irina firmly before slapping her husband on the back of his head while father and daughter continued to stare daggers at each other.

Vitaly struggled to maintain a straight face throughout all this. He'd only just realised how much he'd missed their shenanigans.

"Vitaly has walked all the way here to seek our help!" spat Irina angrily. "The least we could do is behave appropriately," she added, staring daggers herself, first at Anatoly and then Sofia. They both quickly gave way underneath the intensity of her gaze and quickly apologised to Vitaly.

"We received what I'm guessing is a similar letter to the one your family did," stated Anatoly politely and he stood up and walked over to a wooden drawing table. There he opened one of the drawers and withdrew an envelope before returning to his seat at the table.

"Tell me your opinion," he asked Vitaly, sliding the envelope across the table to his nephew.

Vitaly picked it up and slowly opened it before withdrawing the letter inside. He knew straight away what it was. He recognised the Soviet emblem immediately. The sickle and hammer on a globe depicted in the rays of the sun and framed by ears of wheat with the inscription "proletarians of the world unite." Karasev and his men had all worn pins on their breasts depicting the same symbol.

"Yes, that is the same letter, Uncle," replied Vitaly reluctantly while offering a reassuring smile.

"Remind me of the date of their visit, Vitaly. It's written there at the top," said his uncle, pointing to the letter.

"Twenty-ninth of July," replied Vitaly.

"And what's the date today?" enquired his uncle thoughtfully.

"It's the twenty-eighth!" replied Irina with alarm, and Anatoly, Irina and Sofia looked from one another to Vitaly, fear and concern covering their faces.

"What!? No!" replied a very resigned Vitaly and he looked back at them imploringly before dropping the letter to the table. "What should I do? Should I leave? Do I run away again?" he asked, panic rising in his voice as he looked out through the window at the receding afternoon sunlight.

"No, no, it's okay, Vitaly," came his uncle's reply and he patted his nephew's hand supportively. "You should stay tonight and rest your leg. Besides, it's getting late and as long as you're not here when they arrive in the morning, you should have nothing to worry about," he added with a forced smile.

"What time are they arriving?" asked Irina before Anatoly grabbed the letter and quickly scanned through it for the answer.

"Eight a.m.," He replied.

"Then your uncle is right!" replied Irina firmly, nodding her head in approval of the idea. "You need rest and a hot meal, and I certainly won't be sending my nephew away unnecessarily," she added, smiling warmly.

"Thank you," came Vitaly's croaky and relieved reply. He looked on his aunt and uncle warmly, any thought of any lingering anger directed towards him for the loss of their son vanished as quickly as the seconds passed. Drowning in affection and sentiment, he quickly looked away as a tear creased his cheek.

He rubbed his right eye and gave a slight sniffle before turning back to them. "Will you excuse me? I need a cigarette," he said softly.

"Of course," replied his uncle enthusiastically.

Vitaly rose as the three sets of eyes watched him carefully. He walked purposely towards his bag and withdrew his tobacco and papers before turning back to the table. "If you don't mind, I'm going outside," he said softly, and they all caught the implication of his wanting to be alone.

He stepped through the doorway to the mumbled sounds of his extended family's continued conversation. He didn't want to hear it. He knew it would be laced with nothing but worry and concern so he walked down the stairs and across the yard to the dairy.

There, he leaned on the wooden gate and opened his tobacco pouch and rolled himself a cigarette. Lighting it, he inhaled deeply and looked up into the darkening blue sky. Several stars were already visible and, searching closer to the horizon, he located the slowly rising moon.

"Vitaly?" came his cousin's feminine voice, causing him to jump. He hadn't heard her approaching footsteps.

"Damn it, Sofia! You frightened me!" he replied with

annoyance as he turned to find his cousin crossing the yard towards him.

"Can I talk to you?" she asked hesitantly.

Vitaly looked at her with suspicion as she joined him, coming to a stop in front of him in the shadow of the barn. It was clearly evident to him how nervous she was.

"What about?" he asked, a little too aggressively. Sofias expression indicated she was not impressed by his tone, so, with a considerable increase in sensitivity, he asked again. "What about?"

"Edgar Tarlov," she replied, staring into his eyes defiantly.

"Listen, I'm not talking about the war, okay!?" he shot back savagely. "So, give it a rest!" he added before turning away and resting his arms again on the gate.

"It's not about the war," came her firm reply.

"Bullshit!" he shot back without looking at her and between drags on his cigarette.

"Vitaly, it's not. I swear!" came her pleading reply and he noticed her tone had changed. He turned to look at her. She looked sad, almost on the verge of tears. Feeling guilty, he gestured for her to join him.

"Okay, Sofia, what is it then?"

"Edgar Tarlov has asked me to marry him," she stated quickly and Vitaly was completely caught off guard. He turned his head to look at his little cousin, all of seventeen years old, beautiful as she was feisty. She smiled back at him sweetly.

"Wow!" was all he could reply and she giggled affectionately.

"I know," she said, continuing to smile almost foolishly before holding out her arms as if to say, look at me.

Composing himself, Vitaly said, "And what was your reply?" and handed her his cigarette in a sign of solidarity. She puffed on it before handing it back to him, the look upon her face full of sadness. He felt confused so he pulled his flask out of his pocket and unscrewed the lid and offered it to her.

"This helps," he said softly before offering a weak yet understanding smile, and she drank.

"You heard Papa in there," she stated. "He doesn't approve."

"Have you asked him?" asked Vitaly thoughtfully.

"No," she stated bluntly. "I'm afraid he'll say no and I'll be forced to run away."

"You're that serious about this Edgar?" asked Vitaly, surprised. He looked at his little cousin with intrigue.

"Yes!" she replied with conviction. "He's lovely. He's going to be a doctor and move to Moscow and maybe later on overseas. And I want to marry him and join him and see the world!" she exclaimed passionately as her eyes became watery. "I don't want to be another farmer's wife and never leave Kyrubol."

"Okay. And you're afraid to ask your father and be told no and then have to run away and break your parents' hearts?" asked Vitaly with surprising certainty.

"Yes!" she replied, relieved. "You understand! I knew you would understand!" she added before throwing her arms around her cousin in a grateful embrace.

"I tell you what, Sofia," replied Vitaly softly as he patted her on the back gently. "Let me finish my cigarette and have a few swigs of vodka for courage before we head inside and you tell your parents that you've received a marriage proposal which you're going to accept."

"Okay." She mumbled in reply, sniffling into his shoulder. She let him go and he looked at her thoughtfully before speaking again.

"Are you afraid?"

Wiping away a tear, she replied, "Not anymore."

"Well, I'm glad for you because I am," he replied with a serious look.

"Really?" she asked, mimicking Vitaly's expression, which then broke.

"Definitely!" he replied, unable to keep a straight face. "Because compared to the Bolsheviks, uncle Anatoly is a bad, bad man." And he broke out into laughter with Sofia joining him.

"Come on, let's go inside," said Vitaly soothingly and he crushed out his cigarette, took one final swig of his vodka and, putting his arm around his cousin's shoulders, they walked back across the yard to the izba.

A Rude Awakening

The discussion between Sofia and her parents regarding her proposed marriage to Edgar Tarlov had gone surprisingly well, thought Vitaly. As expected, Anatoly had been standoffish at the beginning and while he wouldn't say he had come around exactly, Vitaly theorised that maintaining a good relationship with his daughter and having the privilege of seeing any future grandchildren had been a driving factor in his reluctant acceptance.

Irina on the other hand had been openly pleased at the prospect of her only daughter marrying a doctor. She was an intelligent and pragmatic woman and knew that with the union, Sofia would have an innumerable number of doors opened for her and opportunities presented.

The discussion had been followed by dinner which Vitaly had eaten heartily, exhausted from his day of activities. All four had gone to bed early and Vitaly had fallen asleep quickly but soon enough his dreams had disintegrated and become, once again, disrupted by the usual scenes of felled comrades and human suffering in the battlefield.

It was still dark when his uncle abruptly shook him awake in a panicked state. Initially, Vitaly had thought he was back on the battlefield but quickly recognising his uncle's voice and realised that to be untrue. He could hear movement inside the izba and as his eyes adjusted, he could just make out his uncle's face.

He was leaning over him and pressing his index finger to his lips to indicate silence. Vitaly nodded his understanding despite not knowing if his uncle could see him and they both listened intently. The sound of a car engine outside the izba drew Vitaly's attention immediately. He'd heard the noise in his dream and naturally presumed that's where it had come from.

Now, however, he realised that the sound was coming from outside the izba and immediately became alarmed. This was very suspicious! Very few if any in the village owned a car and fewer still, if they did, would have reason to run it at five in the morning. Vitaly sat up abruptly in alarm but his uncle forced him back down using one hand and again pressed his free index finger to his lips for silence.

"Uncle!" he whispered to Anatoly, who had looked away towards the window.

"Shush," hissed Anatoly without turning to look at him.

"What is it? I can hear a car." Asked Vitaly.

Vitaly looked around the izba and noticed Irina standing by another window and peeking out through the curtain. Sofia remained in her bed but met Vitaly's eyes. She looked frightened.

They could hear voices outside over the low rumble of the engine but it was hard to distinguish what they were saying before a couple of phrases broke through.

"Is this the place?" one asked.

"I think so," replied another before they became indistinguishable again.

There was an elongated moment of silence broken only by the rumble of the engine, which continued without concern for those around asleep in their beds. Then, another phrase broke through.

"Listen, will you cut that damn engine, Nikolai!? Everyone in the village will know we're here, damn it!" came an annoyed voice.

"Sorry boss," was the immediate reply and the engine cut out.

"It's my fault, Kasaev," said the first man sarcastically, his voice now clearly audible. "I forgot that subtlety was not your strong point. They're probably awake now, although I can't see any light coming from inside."

There was silence again and they could hear footsteps approaching the izba from outside. All inside jumped and Irina let out a gasp as one of the men outside pressed his hand to the glass of the window and attempted to peer inside through the curtain.

"See anything, boss?" asked Nikolai casually.

"No. It's pitch-black inside and this curtain's closed," replied the first man, the one referred to by Nikolai as "Boss."

"Can you hear anything?" asked Nikolai, before the boss cupped his hand and pressed his ear against the glass.

Anatoly quickly looked to Irina then Sofia and back whilst continuing to press his index finger to his lips. He pressed so hard this time, Vitaly could see his lips turn visibly white through the darkness.

"A negative on that one too I'm afraid," replied the Boss.

They listened carefully as the boss took several footsteps away from the window before they let out a collective sigh of relief. Irina tentatively peered through the curtain again. In front of her, upon the cool glass, she could clearly see the smudged marks left by the stranger's cupped hand. A car door closed, indicating the second man, Kasaev, had exited the vehicle and joined the boss prowling around outside the izba.

"I think it's time to go, Vitaly," came Anatoly's hushed voice. He removed his hand from his nephew's chest. "Get dressed, grab your bag and gun – and do it quietly," he added whilst looking again towards the window.

Vitaly followed his uncle's order without hesitation and hastily threw his blanket back before dropping his legs down over the side of the cot. He had slept in his underwear so he quickly pulled on his pants and shirt before pulling on his boots. He then bent down and reached beneath the cot to grab his bag and rifle.

Vitaly banged his head against the frame of the cot as Irina and Sofia each emitted a loud gasp in response to the thunderous bang upon the front door. Vitaly was seeing stars as his uncle grabbed him and roughly ushered him to the rear door.

"Hello, comrades!" came the boss's booming voice. "Is there anyone inside? I am a representative of the local Soviet. Please open the door. I have some questions to ask you regarding your nephew, Vitaly Petrovich Borisov."

"Well, I thought as much," exclaimed Anatoly derisively. "You wait until I answer the door," he explained firmly to Vitaly, who was rubbing the back of his head tenderly. "I'll step outside and take their attention. Then you go out this door and into the woods. Okay?" He looked more serious than Vitaly had ever seen him.

"Yes, Uncle," Vitaly agreed quietly before they shook hands.

"There, now, get ready," said Anatoly, pointing at the back door before he turned and walked away towards the front one. Vitaly nodded a silent farewell to his aunt and cousin before very carefully opening the door and half stepping through. With bag over shoulder and rifle in hand, he was cautious to ensure there was nobody standing on the other side in ambush. He heard the click of the latch and stepped further out, slowly closing the door behind him as his uncle slowly opened the other. Then he heard his uncle speak.

"What in the hell do you think you're doing!?" barked Anatoly at his very early and very unwelcome visitors.

"I am comrade..." But the voice trailed off as Vitaly descended the stairs and made to cross the farm yard. Suddenly, he sensed a presence by the izba and saw shadowy movement out of the corner of his eye. He didn't bother to look. His goal, his only one, was to make it to the tree line where he could disappear into the darkness of the woods. There he would be safe in the familiar surrounds.

"There's someone here!" yelled Kasaev in surprise.

Vitaly broke into a run, or at least the best attempt his leg would allow. It was stiff from yesterday's journey and ached to no end. He heard raised voices from behind him followed by the crack of a gunshot exploding somewhere overhead. Somehow, he began to move even faster. *I just need to make it to the tree line*, he thought. He could hear his name being called out from behind but he didn't recognise the voice. He wouldn't be turning around to investigate.

Finally, after what felt like forever, he crossed into the cover of the woods. No more shots had been fired. Perhaps they'd given up? But, would they pursue? He automatically presumed so, so he just kept running. He thought he heard more yelling and sensed someone behind him. It might've been the adrenalin but he couldn't stop, wouldn't stop.

His leg had loosened up despite aching now more than ever while sweat poured from his body. Anger and frustration rose at his limitations and he winced at the pain from the stitch stabbing into his ribs. Despite his best efforts his pace slowed before it eventually resembling little more than a hobble.

The very first signs of daylight began to break across the sky above him, signalling another beautiful warm summer's day. The wood remained dark and gloomy however and he tripped on a protruding root and fell at the foot of a diminutive pine. He pounded the ground with the underside of his fist and yelled out with rage.

Rolling over, lungs burning, he inhaled several deep breaths and finally decided that he could go no further. He threw his bag from his back but continued to clutch his rifle firmly. He withdrew his canteen and skulled its contents. Belching, he looked around in confusion. He didn't recognise this place. Anxiety rising, he tried in vain to recall his path but found he couldn't.

He'd obviously taken a wrong turn. One positive thought did cross his mind however, if he didn't know where he was, they probably wouldn't either. While that was comforting, it still wasn't a guarantee of safety.

Resignedly, he knew he needed to keep moving. He certainly needed water and suddenly realised his stomach ached with hunger. So, using every ounce of resilience, he grabbed his bag and willed himself to his feet before setting off again, empty canteen in hand and rifle now slung over his shoulder.

He walked this time, perhaps in circles but with a growing sense of relief as the sun slowly broke through the thick trees above. It grew hotter as the morning matured. Finally, he heard the faint sound of running water somewhere nearby and stumbled around excitedly in search of it. He didn't see the embankment.

He stepped off the edge and tumbled down, somersaulting several times before coming to a rest in a heap at the bottom by the edge of a shallow stream. He groaned in pain before lifting his head and looking at the inviting water. He crawled his way across to it and dunked his entire head beneath the surface before opening his mouth and drinking thirstily. Finally, in need of breath, he sat up before dunking his canteen in and filling it to the brim.

He rose shakily, supporting himself by leaning against the closest tree. He felt dizzy and his temple ached and was tender to his touch. Despite this, he began moving, stumbling around drunkenly and using one tree after another for support. He groggily decided to follow the stream downriver in hopes that it would eventually lead him out into familiar territory.

He'd never felt more fatigued and despite the shade, the summer heat was becoming more and more oppressive. He was increasingly disorientated, dizzy and nauseous so he stopped and looked up through the myriad of branches and observed the bright blue cloudless sky beyond and offered a silent prayer to God.

He could hear the call of several different birds from somewhere above him while the scent of wood and earth filled his nostrils. He refocused his gaze to eye level and waited momentarily for them to readjust to the darker light of the shaded woods. He looked around for somewhere to rest and selected a large fir tree standing nearby.

He walked towards it, limping slightly but crossing the distance quickly. Stopping, he dropped his canteen to the ground before removing his rifle from his shoulder and placing it down against the tree. He then carefully lowered himself into the jumble of cool earth and tree roots next to it.

He made himself comfortable, or as comfortable as possible, before removing his bag and placing it down by his side and withdrawing his tobacco pouch and papers and what was left of his mother's bread and cheese. With great concentration, he placed the tobacco inside the paper, rolled it up, licked and sealed it before inserting the cigarette into his mouth and lighting it.

Inhaling, he closed his eyes and gave a great sigh, satisfaction and relaxation washing over him, and he leaned back against the large trunk. Surely by now the threat had passed, he thought, so it was safe to sit and take a few minutes here to collect his thoughts. After all, here was as good as any spot to rest his aching body.

Despite his eyes being unfocused, he clumsily attempted to inspect himself. His trousers were torn, arms scratched, left elbow bleeding but congealed. He could feel several scratches on his face, one of which stung quite badly. His nose hurt but felt unbroken. His head was a concern but felt better than it had initially after his fall, only continuing to ache slightly. Importantly, nothing appeared to be broken.

He leaned over and rubbed his aching right leg then felt his knee, which had become badly swollen. He began pulling his pant leg up, revealing a long bright pink scar that stretched along the front of his leg from the knee down to the ankle. Once he'd pulled the pant leg up over his knee, he sat back against the trunk again and stared at the scar and slowly became lost in a memory.

It would likely ache for the rest of his life according to the army doctor who had treated him after he'd injured it in the Great War. It wouldn't bend like it used to and to be comfortable he would have to sit and lie with it extended straight out as he did now. The doctor had made it clear that he had been lucky and he knew it. His comrade next to him hadn't been.

The doctor had recommended walking as a remedy. "You must keep it moving," he had said. "Try to imagine you're lubricating a joint." And Vitaly had listened. Working on the farm required an enormous amount of walking and if that wasn't enough, he would take his rifle and wander into the woods behind and around Virubol to hunt game.

Walking had helped enormously and he'd also found that it helped clear his mind. He had noticed too how he would sleep more soundly the night after one of his walks and on particularly arduous days like those spent helping his father on the farm.

He would always take his rifle despite his dislike of guns. Rabbits, hare, ducks, and deer were plentiful and he'd once even shot a large elk. Unfortunately, in his excitement he hadn't comprehended how he would transport the elk pelt home and at the recollection, he smiled to himself with amusement. Ever since, he'd drawn the line at deer which were small enough to carry.

Mama had always been grateful for any extra meat that he or his father could provide. That was the way in rural Siberia. Vitaly had been taught to shoot as a young boy by a combination of his father, grandfather and uncle Anatoly. Evgeny had been taught at the same time.

His mind quickly changed tangents, switching to the feeling of dread he faced every night upon closing his eyes. He could only estimate the number of times he'd vividly relived the moment his comrade had called out to him on the battlefield before suddenly exploding into a haze of wet red mist right in front of his eyes.

He'd never forget that image and the initial incomprehensible fear that he'd lost his leg. However, the most disturbing part wasn't his comrade dying but the experience of being covered in his friend like he was made from some kind of thick red paint. Already nauseous, he felt even worse at the recollection. This is why he couldn't share his story. How could people possibly understand?

In retrospect, Vitaly often felt that his young comrade had been lucky. The unlucky? They, like him, had survived and would now spend their lives living with what they'd seen and done. Many were crippled, having lost limbs, blown off by a shell or gunfire and spread carelessly around the battlefield. Then there were the invisible wounds, wounds that were not evident to the naked eye. Wounds which only vodka helped. Wounds like his.

The snapping of a twig jolted him back to consciousness and he leaned over and rubbed his right knee again absentmindedly. Taking another drag on his cigarette he looked around and observed his surroundings with anxious curiosity. He sensed that he was being watched but surely there was nobody there, not after his escape and not all the way out here. Regardless, he reached for his rifle instinctively.

He still felt thirsty so he drained his canteen in one long skull. He would need more water, so with cigarette in mouth, he took his canteen and rifle and pushed himself up and moved closer to the stream. He stopped at the bank's edge to turn down his pant leg and cover up the hideous scar when suddenly he heard another twig snap and his grip on his gun tightened. He looked up, his pupils dilating and the hairs on his arms standing up as he broke out into goosebumps. Wait, was there somebody there?

"Hello," he called out loudly, and instantly felt foolish. If there was somebody concealed nearby, obviously they wanted it that way. So carefully kneeling on the damp embankment, using the rifle for support and careful to keep a suspicious eye on his surroundings, he plunged his canteen into the stream and filled it part way with cool water.

Between drags on his cigarette, he drank thirstily, quickly emptying the canteen before plunging it back into the stream and partly refilling it again. He repeated this process several times in quick succession before finally, his thirst was quenched and he refilled it fully and started back towards his seat under the fir tree.

As he stood up a small doe appeared from behind a tree several metres away. So that was the source of the noise, he thought to himself, feeling foolish but greatly relieved. He slowly placed his canteen on the ground and swung the rifle up and levelled it at the doe.

Surprisingly, the intrusion of a human into its home caused it no great concern. It simply locked eyes with Vitaly, its big doe eyes staring directly into and through the scope into Vitaly's, which stared directly back. He lined the creature up in the crosshairs and prepared for the kill shot but then its gaze lingered.

Vitaly was overcome with a strange sensation. He felt as if the doe was staring directly into his soul. As if it knew and understood his problems. He considered it for a moment longer. He could use the sustenance of its meat, but he found he couldn't shoot this beautiful, innocent creature. Lowering his weapon, he continued to stare, admiring its beauty before it casually turned and wandered nonchalantly away, leaving him standing there alone with a funny smile on his face.

What was he thinking? He could've killed and eaten it. The bread and cheese his mother had given him wouldn't last long. At the thought of his mother, his mind wandered again. He imagined both her and his father in gaol, arrested for his transgression. He felt strange. He felt his head, wincing as he touched the side of it and suspecting he'd banged it during his tumble earlier.

"You're getting jumpy, old man," he said to himself with a chuckle as he picked up his canteen. He rested his rifle back against the tree before retaking his seat beneath it. He placed his canteen down next to him and reached into his bag to withdraw his flask of vodka. Cigarette still in mouth, he removed the lid on the flask and shotted a generous portion. Replacing the lid securely, he put the flask down carefully next to him.

He leaned back against the trunk, closed his eyes and took one final long drag of his cigarette. He wouldn't tell his father about the doe, he thought. He wouldn't understand – hell, he didn't understand it himself. He'd probably find some rabbits easily enough to compensate. He'd still sleep that night with a full stomach, provided he was still out here.

After several deep breaths he reopened his eyes and crushed his cigarette out on the cool ground before picking up the flask again and raising it before him in a toast to himself. "Nah-zda-rovh-yeh," he mumbled before downing a shot.

It didn't take Vitaly long before he'd downed a second, third, fourth, fifth and sixth, enjoying and savouring each one. After the final one, he suddenly remembered he had miles to walk to get home, if he could go home that was, and he secured the lid of his flask and carefully returned it to his bag.

He'd become sleepy, the vodka having relaxed him and somewhat soothed the combination of soreness and fatigue he felt over his entire body and mind. He didn't fight it, but instead slid down lower against the tree trunk before pulling his cap down over his eyes and quickly drifting off to sleep.

The Dream

Thud, thud, thud. Slowly, rhythmically, thud, thud, thud. Was he dreaming? Surely! Thud, thud, thud. Confused, he opened his eyes and somehow found himself flying. Panicked, he looked from one outstretched arm to the other as he glided high above the ocean beneath him.

He looked down and to his great surprise he could see himself clearly mirrored in the smooth reflection of the water's surface and watched mesmerised as he effortlessly flapped his arms to gain more speed and elevation. His panic subsided because he knew, somehow, that he wasn't going to fall.

Looking to the horizon, he could see land all around, the mountains and cliffs visible far off into the hazy distance. He had no idea where he was or which direction he was heading, but he knew the direction he wanted to go was straight ahead.

The shoreline grew closer, revealing a long thin beach backed by a steep slope which itself was backed by towering stone cliff faces far away in the distance. There was a large white palatial building atop the slope, partially hidden from view behind some thick trees.

He passed over the shoreline and circled. The building was made of white limestone in the neo-renaissance style and seemed to glint in the sunlight. It stood three stories tall and featured Bramantesque windows, an arched portico, a Florentine tower and an Italian courtyard centred on a white marble fountain surrounded by rows of flowers and palm trees.

He circled the Florentine tower, his eyes searching the beautifully manicured grounds below, but for what, he didn't know. At the end of the driveway, directly in front of the structure, stood another larger white marble fountain surrounded by blooming tulips and perfectly manicured hedges.

Continuing to circle, he selected one of the large balconies and descended towards it. His two feet touched the stone floor softly as he landed gracefully. Observing his surroundings, he found he was standing in an opulent sunlit balcony surrounded by jasper vases. The scent of wood and earth was gone, replaced by the aroma of the sea which he inhaled deeply.

There was a large ornate wrought-iron couch resting up against a stone wall and he decided to lie down upon it. Lying on his back, hands resting behind his head, they sunk softly into the silk pillows beneath. He looking up and yawned carelessly as he observed the white limestone roof above supported by the white marble portico.

The noise continued, thud, thud, thud, and he lifted himself up onto his elbows and looked around with curiosity. Frowning to himself, he dismissed it casually. He half expected it to be a woodpecker hammering away on one of the many nearby trees. Thud, thud, thud, it quickly went again and this time he sat up and looked over the railing, his jaw dropping at the beautiful view below him.

It was the kind of view that made you stand up in

appreciation and in doing so, he stepped towards the stone parapet where his eyes bulged. The ocean stretched out in front of him all the way to the horizon before it met the hillside upon which this impressive structure stood. The foreground was thick with trees and dropped away dramatically to a thin white beach which divided the panorama in two. Thud, thud, thud, the noise came again.

Resting his hands on the wrought iron hand railing, he looked from left to right along the structure in search of its source. He inhaled again deeply, breathing the fresh sea air into his lungs and feeling the cool breeze on his skin. He wondered where he could be when suddenly, a young woman appeared from behind a white marble column and flounced her way towards him, her hips swinging hypnotically.

Turning, he was immediately struck by her beauty. She was young, maybe eighteen or nineteen he thought, with thick long light-brown hair tied up with a single length of red ribbon. Her skin was milk white and blended almost perfectly with her white satin sundress that was tied at the waist with more red ribbon which revealed her curvaceous figure.

Thud, thud, thud. His eyes followed her intently as she joined him at the parapet and gently placed two small feminine hands on the railing. She turned to him and their eyes met. They were a vivid dark blue, like saucers he thought, and danced when she smiled. He was instantly enchanted and became lost in them. Holding his gaze, she flirted playfully, reaching out and touching his arm before taking his hand and giggling innocently at his expression.

"What's wrong, Vitaly?" she asked sweetly, eyes twinkling.

He was in shock. How did this beautiful creature know his name? He offered no coherent response to her question, which caused her to raise her eyebrows in suspicion. So, she asked again, this time more seriously,

"Vitaly, what's wrong?"

"Uh... Where, where am I?" mumbled Vitaly, lost wherever it is in a woman's eyes that a man forgets how to properly articulate words.

The young woman's smile morphed into one of incredulity. Suspecting him of teasing her, playing along, she replied,

"Livadia, silly. In Crimea."

"Oh," he replied simply, unable to break eye contact. But those four words didn't register because he simply couldn't concentrate. She continued to look at him with suspicion before pulling him towards her and then onto the couch and taking a seat beside him. He could feel the warmth of her body against him as she pressed her warm legs against his and stared into his eyes.

"Are you not going to kiss me, Vitaly?" asked the young woman, doe-eyed. "Or are you afraid of my father?" she asked with a serious look before continuing, "Or worse yet, my mother?" She gasped sarcastically, bulging her eyes and sitting up rigidly as if she was being reprimanded.

Vitaly could only stare, entranced at the young beauty before something connected in his mind. He'd seen this woman before, of that he was certain. But where?

She leaned closer, eyes dancing as she held his gaze. The heat radiating between them intensified as their noses touched and a stray strand of light-brown hair fell down around her face, brushing his. He was weak. He knew it. He wasn't going to be able to resist her advance and cared little at this moment of her name or who she and her parents were.

Thud, thud, thud. It was that noise again. He'd forgotten about it or just merely shut it out, distracted as he had become by this girl. Perhaps it was his heart? he thought. It was beating that hard he wouldn't have been surprised if she could hear it.

All thoughts of it disappeared again as finally, their lips met and it was ecstasy. Their eyes closed before Vitaly brushed his hand softly across her rosy cheek then upwards to her temple and finally into her hair, intimately. The tables had turned; she was now at his mercy.

Thud, thud, thud came the noise again. Was it getting louder? Surely it was his heart. No, it couldn't be. It was that strange noise. He really couldn't be sure and at this moment didn't really care. Time had momentarily stood still until, regaining their senses, their lips parted and they embraced. The young woman pushed Vitaly back onto the couch and then lay herself on top of him, entwining herself in his arms.

THUD, THUD, THUD it came once again and much louder than before. Okay, that definitely wasn't his heart, unless it was about to violently burst from his chest.

"Did you hear that?" he asked her, very seriously.

"Hear what?" she replied innocently, head resting on his chest and rising in rhythm with his breaths as the cool sea breeze moved through her hair and ruffled it lightly.

THUD, THUD, THUD.

He raised himself onto his elbows, forcing her to sit up. Disgruntled, she frowned at him.

"I was comfortable," she said with exasperation.

"Did you not hear that, girl?" he asked again, this time more forcibly, panic rising within him while he looked around for the source.

"I didn't hear anything," she replied indignantly, "besides the sound of the wind in the trees and waves crashing on the beach. Also, please don't call me girl. I have a name!"

"And what is that?" he asked, panicked, as the room suddenly began to swim, the outlines becoming fuzzy like an unfocused photograph. At the same time sound become distorted. She was speaking but he couldn't make out her words. Despite listening intently, all he could make out were "marriage" and "love" or "I love" but that was it. Was she saying that she loved him?

THUD, THUD, THUD.

He forced her off him as he shot up from the couch like a bolt of lightning. Leaning over the parapet, he searched the grounds below expectantly but there was nothing there. THUD, THUD, THUD it came again, and this time the whole building shook, violently as if from an earthquake. He turned to her, panic etched on his face, while hers remained a mask of intrigue mixed with sadness.

THUD, THUD, THUD, and she suddenly stood up and rushed towards him. She embraced him tightly, wrapping her arms around his waist before looking up into his eyes.

"Please don't go, Vitaly. Please don't wake up. Stay here with me," she said softly as tears began to fill her eyes. THUD, THUD, THUD.

Realisation washed over him. It was only a dream, he remembered now. But what a sweet dream! He didn't want to leave but in reality, he was still sitting under a tree in the woods alone, tired, battered and bruised. Calming himself, he looked into her blue eyes and smiled before kissing her passionately. As he did the building shook again.

When their lips finally parted, he stared longingly into her eyes before he spoke. "I'm afraid this is only a dream, my dear," he said, the sadness and disappointment evident in every syllable. He then looked up and around at the building as it began to crumble around them.

Looking into her eyes again, he added, "I assure you it's been a sweet dream. Possibly the sweetest one I've ever had," and he smiled. "And I really don't want to leave," he said as the building shook again, this time even more violently than before. He tenderly brushed a tear from her cheek before pulling her back close to him. There she nestled her head under his chin as he smelled her hair.

Suddenly, as quickly as a snap of the fingers, the image dissolved before him, taking the young woman with it and leaving Vitaly holding nothing but air. He stood in complete darkness and noticed the scent of the ocean had gone too, replaced with the familiar scent of wood and earth. He awoke abruptly, disappointed to find himself once again sitting under the fir tree and lost deep inside the Siberian Forest.

The Stranger

He was overcome with confusion and squinted his eyes in response to the abrupt change in light. The back of his head ached, his back and legs too. He had momentarily forgotten where he was and why he was here, then it all came rushing back and he was enveloped in disappointment and defeat.

His eyes adjusted and he was finally able to look around comfortably. He noticed his cap was gone and that his canteen had moved, lying now discarded on the ground next to him while the bread and cheese remained exactly where he had left them.

He couldn't have been asleep that long, maybe an hour, although probably less. It was a guess though, made in judgment of the distance and angle of the shadows made by the sun which now rested near the middle of the sky indicating midday.

Closing his eyes to the light, he placed his hands to his forehead, straining as he did with the effort to remember the dream. The girl's face swam behind his closed eyes, the clarity of her image decreasing with every passing second. He knew her, he had to, she just looked so familiar. How frustrating it was to have the answer on the tip of one's tongue.

But where do I know her from? he thought. Maybe a girl from his village? Perhaps one he had once shared a classroom with? Or was she the younger sister of a class mate? "Stupid memory," he uttered softly with disgust.

Despite still feeling groggy, he placed his hand against the tree for support as he pushed himself up. He grimaced from the pain that shot through his body as he stood and stretched out his arms above him before emitting a long yawn. He felt his left elbow tenderly and licked his fingers before trying to use his saliva to wipe away the blood that had dried there.

He bent down, retrieving his canteen from the ground and placing it back inside his bag which he then lifted and hung over his shoulder. He looked around for his cap and circled the tree slowly in hopes of finding it. No luck there, so he inspected the contents of his bag and was again disappointed.

Thud, thud, thud came that familiar sound and his heart skipped a beat. He shot around in alarm to face the direction from which he thought it had come and instinctively reached for his rifle. It had reverberated through the densely packed woods so perhaps he was mistaken, so he waited anxiously for it to come again.

Thud, thud, thud. and there it was as if on cue, faint but still managing to carry through the stillness of the forest. It was coming from the direction he faced, which was downstream. He narrowed his eyes and searched the distance but it must be far off, out of sight and obscured by the trees.

He adjusted the strap of his bag and took a deep breath. He distinctly remembered it from his dream and at the recollection a combination of adrenalin and curiosity took control of his senses. Thud, thud, thud, the noise continued, barely audible over the sound of the flowing stream.

Should he follow it and discover its source? It could be dangerous! Potentially yes, and he looked down at himself and reflected upon his physical state. He calmly rationalised that perhaps it was a side effect from the hit to the head, or maybe he was simply imagining it? Thud, thud, thud, it came again and the explosion of birdsong from above convinced him otherwise.

They can hear it too, he thought. Therefore, it must be real and he looked up into the branches appreciatively. Looking back down, he bent down and picked up his bread and cheese before brushing away several small ants and devouring it.

Thud, thud, thud. What could it be? A woodpecker was the most obvious choice and he imagined one hammering away on a pine tree. Into his mind came another image, a humorous and thoroughly unlikely one which made him smile. A bear using a hammer? He imagined a Siberian Brown hammering in a nail. But they didn't venture this far west, he reasoned, before shaking his head and dismissing the idea completely because they couldn't use hammers.

What about a woodcutter? He doubted it very much. Few if any people ventured into these woods. They knew better, not that there was any real danger unless you count the nonsense story his grandfather had told him about Baba Yaga. These rural peasants were surprisingly superstitious though. No, he eliminated a woodcutter from the list of possibilities, Baba Yaga too.

Finally, deciding that he would simply go and find out, he readjusted his bag and tightened his grip on his rifle. He was optimistic that this direction would lead him to a road or pathway and then out of the forest. His water supply was safe as long as he stayed close to the stream but his food was now completely gone so he couldn't really remain here regardless. So, absent of other options, he set off.

The sound became spasmodically drowned out by the crunch of his footsteps as he began moving stiffly towards it, blindly, as if in some bizarre game of Marco Polo. He walked on for several minutes, following the stream which appeared to be leading him directly to the sound's source, indicated by the gradual increase in volume.

He stumbled on broken tree branches and tripped over an exposed tree root, twisting his ankle in the process and causing him even more pain. His bloodied elbow began to bleed again upon impact with the ground and he ripped another hole in his trousers, revealing the horrible scarring on his leg.

Oh, how he longed for his soft cot in the izba in Virubol. Yet, despite these obstacles laid down by mother nature, he continued on determinedly while cautiously pausing every few minutes or so to gauge his surroundings and to listen.

He came to another stop, thud, thud, thud, and peered through the trees which had finally begun to thin. He could now see into a clearing beyond their edge. He slowed his pace as he drew closer, careful to be quiet and remain concealed until he discovered the sound's source.

There was movement beyond, to which he reacted instinctively, quickly taking refuge behind a particularly thick pine while careful to remain as silent as possible. After taking several deep breaths, he cautiously peeked around the trunk's edge and was relieved to find it was a man. Although he now wondered what else he'd expected despite having earlier ruled it out as a possibility.

Vitaly's first thought was, clearly this man didn't believe the tale of Baba Yaga. The second, randomly popping back into his head, was of the bear using a hammer and he smiled to himself again, grateful that nobody had been around with whom he could've shared such a foolish idea.

The man stood in the clearing, his back to Vitaly. He'd

stopped doing whatever it was he'd been doing. He removed his hat and appeared to wipe his brow before drinking thirstily from a canteen. After replacing the lid, he dropped it to the ground beside him then bent down, his hand reaching for something else lying in the grass.

It was an axe. Not a woodpecker, gun, earthquake or most foolishly, a bear with a hammer. Thud, thud, thud, the sound recommenced, once again reverberating through the woods. He must be a woodcutter then, or merely a peasant collecting firewood in anticipation of winter, Vitaly thought.

After silently watching him for several minutes, Vitaly concluded that the man must be out here all alone. A solitary figure, much like himself, deep inside the woods. The only difference was, this stranger wasn't lost. There was a single Vyatka horse tied up next to the stream in the shade of a small pine tree and a small wheeled troika parked nearby. Another small wagon behind it was filled with neatly stacked firewood.

Vitaly continued to watch the man, deciding as he did so what he would do next. He couldn't help but be impressed with the stranger's work ethic and suspected that he must be young, perhaps the same age as Vitaly. He appeared to be enjoying himself as he split felled logs into smaller blocks and then carried them over and stacked them onto the small wagon. His sleeves were rolled back, revealing well-defined and tanned forearms and Vitaly suspected that beneath his shirt was a lean yet muscular physique not that dissimilar to his own.

Wanting a closer look, Vitaly raised his rifle to observe the stranger through its scope. In actuality and to Vitaly's surprise, his magnified profile revealed a man of middle age, average height, light build and sporting a small moustache and short beard. Again, using the scope, Vitaly searched the stranger's proximity for any weapons including rifles and pistols but found nothing.

He didn't look like a Bolshevik, if it was possible to define what a Bolshevik looked like. He at least didn't have a Soviet badge pinned to his chest like Karasev had, which in these circumstances was good enough for Vitaly. He also didn't recognise him but perhaps he would up close, which by then would be too late. Would he recognise Vitaly? That was what Vitaly was afraid of.

Deciding to err on the side of caution, he continued watching the man for several more minutes, alternating between his naked eye and the rifle scope. Finally, more out of curiosity than anything, he decided that yes, he would walk out and introduce himself. Besides, there was no reason this stranger wouldn't be friendly. The war was over. Plus, he might have some extra food, tobacco or even some vodka.

At that thought, Vitaly drew a deep breath before confidently stepping out from concealment behind the thick pine. Walking brusquely, gun in hand, he covered the distance to the tree line quickly before one last wave of reticence washed over him and caused him to hesitate and his pace to slow.

Breathing deeply again, he was able to suppress his anxiety and with a single yet considerably deep swallow, before he knew it, he had stepped out of the cool dark woods and into the clearing and bright sunshine beyond.

The Invitation

The man didn't hear Vitaly approaching. With his back to him, axe in hand, he'd recommenced splitting blocks before the axe became stuck in a particularly uncooperative one, causing the man to swear angrily.

Vitaly instantly feared he'd misjudged the situation and stranger so he stopped cautiously several feet behind him. The hand holding his rifle hurt and had turned white with the pressure he was exerting on the weapon as he waited for an opening between thuds to greet the stranger. "Hello," he finally called, though tentatively.

As if struck by lightning, the man literally jumped with fright, which if the situation hadn't been so tense, Vitaly would have found uproariously amusing. Upon landing, he spun around, in the process losing his grip on the axe which then came flying towards Vitaly. Luckily, aided by adrenalin and his heightened senses, Vitaly's reflexes were taut with anticipation. He quickly ducked and easily avoided the axe as it flew over his head and landed on the grass behind him with a loud thud.

Vitaly, feet now rooted to the spot, looked around at the axe before turning back to the man. Their eyes locked and after several rapid breaths, the man spat angrily in Russian, "You fool! What's the idea of you sneaking up behind me like that? Are you trying to give me a heart attack!?"

"I'm sorry, comrade, I didn't mean to frighten you. I uh, I, I didn't know how else to approach you," Vitaly replied sheepishly.

"Well, you failed miserably!" the man spat angrily. "What were you doing hiding in the woods?" he asked savagely, despite noticing and now attentively watching the rifle in Vitaly's hand.

"I wasn't hiding, comrade," pleaded Vitaly. "I was walking before I took a rest and fell asleep. I was awoken by the sound of your axe, which I then followed to find you here."

Observing Vitaly with intensity, the man replied, "Walking in the woods!? Really!? It's a long way to the nearest village from here! Also, in my experience, walking is made considerably easier when you're not carrying a rifle," he added sarcastically while continuing to eyeball Vitaly's gun suspiciously. "So, what are you really doing out here?"

"I'm afraid I'm lost, comrade," explained Vitaly. "That's all. That's why I'm here," he added with a self-deprecating smile.

"Oh, you're lost, are you?" asked the stranger derisively, sneering before flashing his own disbelieving smile and nodding his head mockingly.

"Yes, comrade, that's all," Vitaly replied defensively. "I've come from Virubol where my family has a farm." He pointed his thumb over his shoulder to indicate its direction although in truth, from here he wasn't sure what direction it was in.

The stranger didn't reply and his silence made Vitaly uneasy. "I walk these woods regularly, have done for years, but today I must've taken a wrong turn," he explained with a nervous laugh. "Also, I carry this rifle out of necessity despite having had more than enough of them during the war," he continued, hopefully, but again received no reply besides that suspicious stare.

"Um, I also hunt small game. You know how it is out here in the country?" he asked, indicating his rifle. "You've got to help feed your family however you can," he finished, hoping that the stranger would finally understand.

The man's expression did change, finally morphing, much to Vitaly's surprise, into one of amusement. Then he spoke. "What the hell have you been hunting that's left you looking like that?" he asked, noticing Vitaly's ragged and battered condition.

Vitaly, inspecting himself again, thought carefully before replying. He brushed some dirt from the front of his torn trousers and held up his bloodied elbow. He didn't want to lie, especially if the stranger was willing to help him.

"I wasn't hunting," he replied. "As I explained, I became lost before attempting to find my way out. In the process I've fallen over, hit my head, twisted my ankle, hurt my elbow and scratched, well, everything," he explained with exasperation before raising his arms in defeat.

The stranger continued to smile with amusement, much to Vitaly's annoyance.

"My predicament isn't funny, comrade," he spat, his temper rising. "You interrogate me but what about you? What are you doing out here?"

The man continued to stare intently, although he remained silent. His expression had changed again, this time indicating alarm at Vitaly's aggressive outburst. Vitaly was suddenly reminded of yesterday's meeting with Karasev. He couldn't risk that happening again so after a deep breath, he relented.

"I'm sorry, comrade," he said calmly, nodding his head

lightly and forcing a smile. He hoped this would somehow make the stranger understand. Thankfully, and again surprisingly, it had the desired effect and the man's face slackened as suspicion was replaced by curiosity.

"You fought for Russia in the Great War? You fought against the Germans?" asked the man with interest. Vitaly was taken back by the question and laughed loudly, alarming two nearby hen harriers and causing them to take flight from their tree, their blue and white feathers blending with the sky seamlessly.

"Yes," he replied pleasantly, relieved at the change of subject. "On the Eastern Front."

"Was my question somehow funny?" asked the man with confusion, his face displaying the faintest trace of disgust.

"No, not at all, comrade," Vitaly replied before quickly explaining himself. "It's just that for a second there I thought we were going to fight and I would be forced to shoot you, and the next you're asking me about the war," he finished, casually shrugging his shoulders and smiling with amusement.

The stranger looked back, clearly still confused. Taking a moment, he considering Vitaly's reply before he too broke into a smile. "Oh yes, I see it now," he chuckled appreciatively. "I do apologise for the alarm but you frightened me," he added.

"In the future I must remember not to approach a wood cutter from behind when they're holding an axe," said Vitaly, chuckling.

"Yes, I wouldn't recommend it," replied the stranger with a laugh. "You were lucky today," he added.

"Just to check, we're not going to fight?" asked Vitaly in jest as he displayed a wry smile.

"No, I don't think so. I certainly don't see the necessity of it," replied the man with another chuckle. "However, I too desire confirmation. You're not going to shoot me, are you? I am unarmed, besides my trusty axe there in the grass behind you, that is."

"No, I don't think so. Certainly not today," said Vitaly, shaking his head before they both laughed pleasantly at having avoided disaster.

"So, you fought in the war?" the man asked again, the tension having broken.

"That is correct, comrade."

"What about after the war? Did you join the Bolsheviks and fight for the Reds under Lenin against the Whites? Or did you remain a loyal monarchist?"

Taken off guard by the question, Vitaly paused for a moment to think about it. That was a potentially dangerous one to ask a stranger, especially here in Siberia which had been a Bolshevik stronghold. Why did he have to ask it? They'd just become agreeable and now he was jeopardising that.

"I've never considered myself a monarchist," replied Vitaly, apprehensively. "I fought for Russia in the Great War, not the Czar. I got swept up in the revolution after being injured on the Eastern Front. It was during my convalescence that my comrades first mutinied. I didn't join them immediately, I couldn't, not until I'd recovered, by which time they'd already marched into Petrograd. Then I joined the Bolsheviks, at least for the time being."

"Only for a time?" asked the man curiously, raising his eyebrows. He had followed Vitaly's words with a childlike fascination.

"I stood for the cause but found myself unable to stand with their methods," Vitaly replied with sadness. "Some of the revolutionaries behaved worse than animals," he added bitterly, spitting on the ground in front of him. "Did you fight?"

"I was in Mogilev," replied the man. "It was decided that I was too old to fight at the front so instead I served in a noncombatant role. A mere administrator for the generals and the Czar."

"The Czar?" asked Vitaly with surprise, before adding, "Did you meet him?"

"I've met him and spoken to him. Both times being at Mogilev," the stranger replied casually.

"Have you heard the rumours?" asked Vitaly.

"What rumours?" replied the stranger, his forehead creased in concentration.

"That the Czar and his family, the Czarina, Czarevich and Grand Duchesses were all murdered by the Bolsheviks on Lenin's orders?"

"Hmmm, sadly, yes," the man replied solemnly before Vitaly interjected.

"Also, several of his uncles, nephews, his own brother Grand Duke Michael and the Czarina's sister, Grand Duchess Elizabeth."

"Yes, I've heard that too."

"If it's true, what those animals did to him and his family is disgusting," stated Vitaly passionately, the stranger looking on with intrigue.

"I thought you weren't a monarchist?" He asked.

"You don't have to be a monarchist to appreciate unnecessary brutality," Vitaly replied sharply. "Murdering the czar is one thing but the women and children? That is unforgivable and one of the many reasons why I abandoned Bolshevism. It's disgraceful."

"I completely agree," replied the man. He offered Vitaly an understanding smile which dually conveyed his satisfaction with his point of view. "What's your name, comrade?"

"Vitaly," replied Vitaly as the man stepped forward and stretched out his hand for a handshake.

"My name is Feliks," he said with a warm smile, releasing

Vitaly's hand, "and again, I apologise," he added. "You don't get many people out this way so you must forgive my surprise."

"It's understandable, Feliks," replied Vitaly, pleased at the conversation's outcome and waving off Feliks concerns genially.

"Are you badly injured?" asked Feliks, looking him up and down.

"Not too badly, I don't think," he replied, lifting his arm and inspecting his bloodied elbow again. "Nothing feels broken but I was dizzy earlier and my eyesight was blurred after I fell and hit my head."

Feliks looked at him with concern before inspecting his head and noticing the large red welt on his temple. Standing this close, the smell of vodka on Vitaly's breath had become noticeable.

"Anything else?" asked Feliks softly.

"Just some scratches and bruises," replied Vitaly dismissively. "Thankfully my mother is a competent seamstress, otherwise it would be the end for these trousers."

"The bruise on your temple looks nasty, Vitaly. I'm no doctor, but I would suggest having it examined."

"I'll take your advice just as soon as I'm back in Virubol," replied Vitaly, unconcerned.

"I don't know," exclaimed Feliks, worriedly looking over Vitaly again.

I'm fine, thought Vitaly; the dizziness and blurred vision had subsided. The headache remained, but that could be a combination of vodka and dehydration.

"Can I make another suggestion?" asked Feliks seriously, continuing before Vitaly could interrupt. "My two oldest daughters are trained nurses. They are back at my izba as we speak. It's only a couple of kilometres from here through the woods," he pointed in the direction of a rough track that disappeared between an overgrown avenue of trees at the edge of the clearing. "They could take a look at you."

Vitaly looked into Feliks' eyes and inspected his face. Once again, there was familiarity there but Vitaly dismissed it. Should he accompany him? This stranger seemed genuine. He possessed kind eyes, evident now that they were up close and on friendlier terms.

"No, it's okay," replied Vitaly. "I don't want to intrude."

"It would be no intrusion," Feliks assured him, waving his hand dismissively. "Besides, my daughters would appreciate the change in company," he added with a smile which was followed by a reassuring nod. "Also, are you hungry?"

Vitaly broke into his own smile and nodded back enthusiastically. "Always," he replied, causing Feliks to laugh.

"Very good, very good," said Feliks, nodding appreciatively. "Like other men I know your stomach takes precedence over your health. In that case and as it's growing late, would you care to join my family and I for dinner? I would be interested to hear more about your service to Russia during the war, and I'm sure my daughters would too."

"I, yes, okay, sure," stumbled Vitaly, surprised at this unforeseeable turn of events and his stomach growling with approval. "I would very much like to join you and your family for dinner."

"Excellent!" replied Feliks, clapping his hands together. "May I ask you for one small favour though in exchange for my hospitality?"

"Yes, comrade," replied Vitaly nervously, nodding but failing to disguise his apprehensiveness.

"It's okay, I only desire your help to load the last of this wood onto my cart. It's only over there," he pointed towards the cart, troika and horse in the shade by the nearby stream. "I'll hitch the horse while you do, if that's alright?"

"Yes, that's perfectly fine," replied Vitaly, feeling relieved, before sliding his bag off his shoulder and dropping it onto the ground and placing his rifle down next to it. Within several seconds his arms were stacked full with as many blocks as he could carry.

"Thank you, my friend," replied Feliks, patting Vitaly on his shoulder gently. "My old back isn't what it used to be," he added before turning and walking towards his horse and troika.

It only took a few minutes for the two men to complete the task and once having done so they collected up their belongings, Vitaly's bag and rifle and Feliks discarded axe and canteen and slid them beneath the seat of the troika before climbed aboard.

Once comfortable, Feliks removed a small silver cigarette case from his pocket, opened it and offered one to Vitaly, who despite sweating profusely, gladly accepted. After removing one for himself Feliks returned the case to his pocket before removing some matches.

Vitaly leaned over as Feliks lit his cigarette, the two men's faces coming close together. This time, Vitaly really focused his attention to the man's face. He was familiar. Very familiar! Of distinction was a faded scar, eight or nine centimetres long running along the right side of his forehead and although he didn't ask, he was curious as to the circumstances with which he had acquired it.

Leaning back, Felix lit his own cigarette then waved out the match and returned the rest to his pocket. Taking the reins, he looked at Vitaly, smiled reassuringly then released the break and yelled "Hyah." And they were away.

The Girl

Feliks drove the troika slowly out of the clearing and into the shaded woods, following the narrow path marked by two rutted wheel tracks and lined with broken branches and tree roots.

"The road is bumpy," said Vitaly, breaking the silence after exhaling a mouthful of smoke and pleased to have his hatless head out of the hot sun. Using his forearm, he wiped away the sweat dripping from his forehead.

"Yes, you had best hold on," replied Feliks as the troika's wheel crunched over a fallen branch then rolled over a protruding tree root, bouncing the two men in their seats. "I imagine I'm the only one who uses it. In fact, despite my daughters, you're the first person I've seen out here. Help yourself to my canteen," he added, having noticed Vitaly wipe his brow.

"Thank you but I have my own," he replied gratefully, reaching for his bag beneath the seat and removing the canteen before opening it and drinking from it thirstily. His leg ached. In this position he couldn't fully extend it so between mouthfuls he tried distracting himself. He looked at Feliks with curiosity. "Have you always lived out here?" he asked as Feliks took a long drag on his cigarette.

Exhaling, Feliks turned to Vitaly, looking him clear in the eye. Vitaly stared back, transfixed by those kind blue-grey eyes. Removing the cigarette from his mouth, Feliks replied, "Several years now." He smiled kindly. "My wife and son, they were sick when we came here and I had no interest in fighting my Russian brothers in a bloody civil war. So instead, I brought them here to escape the conflict."

Vitaly noticed Feliks' use of the past tense to reference his wife and son and how, upon mention of them his facial expression had changed. His eyes too, went from attentive and kind to distant and sad. He turned away from Vitaly and returned the cigarette to his mouth before fiddling with his cap restlessly, seemingly adjusting it to a more comfortable position.

"I can't imagine a safer or more secluded place," said Vitaly between sips of water. "Although, regarding your wife and son's illnesses, the location I imagine would be troublesome for attaining medical attention, certainly of the urgent kind. Although, if your daughters are nurses it's probably not as important…"

"My late wife, she was also a trained nurse," exclaimed Feliks softly. "Two nurses under the one roof are more than adequate, let alone three," he added, turning to Vitaly and smiling again pleasantly.

"You know, there's no doctor in Virubol, nor in Kyrubol to my knowledge, which I'm guessing is closer to here than Virubol," stated Vitaly.

"Honestly, I'm not sure, my friend," replied Feliks casually. "I would need a map to check."

"Anyway, at home, we are visited monthly by a doctor who travels from Ekaterinburg," explained Vitaly.

"Hmm, I think, yes, I believe Kyrubol is closer and I believe it is visited by the same doctor," replied Feliks with uncertainty.

Vitaly, attempting not to stare at and make Feliks feel uncomfortable, chanced several sideways glances at his new friend between further swigs from the canteen before, thirst quenched, he replaced the stopper and dropped the canteen back into his bag and placed it back beneath their seat. Meanwhile, Feliks remained silent and focused on the road ahead, which now split in two.

"Which way?" asked Vitaly pleasantly, again breaking the silence and attempting to keep the conversation flowing.

"We turn left," replied Feliks, and sure enough with a gentle pull on the reins the little Vyatka steered the troika in that direction and continued onwards leisurely. "We follow the stream home," said Feliks softly but reassuringly, pointing to his left into the woods. "We lose sight of it, however it's just behind those trees."

"Where does it flow to?" asked Vitaly curiously, leaning forward to look at the vanishing stream as it became obscured by a collection of pine trees.

Feliks, mishearing him, replied, "We re-join it shortly, just up ahead on the road. That's where my home is, on the edge of a field just west of its confluence with the Tura River. It's a beautiful place." Feliks dropped his cigarette onto the troika's floor and crushed it out with his foot. Vitaly copied him shortly afterwards.

"It's about two kilometres from home to the clearing," he stated, pointing back over his shoulder to indicate where they had come from. "So, it makes collecting easy."

Vitaly found himself admiring the beauty of the woods as

they continued to roll along leisurely. As he looked around, he became extremely conscious of how quickly his line of vision became hampered by the many varying types of trees and other obstructions that filled this beautiful landscape.

Before long, as Feliks had stated, the stream reappeared on their left and the woods began to thin. It was now mid-afternoon, Vitaly guessed by looking at the sky, which in Siberia at the height of summer meant there was still several hours of sunlight left in the day.

The road straightened and the stream came to its edge, lapping at an eroded bank. To Vitaly, it appeared that with snow melt or merely heavy rain, the roadway would easily become flooded. Ahead, he could see a green field and spotted a stone chimney set with clay through the trees. From it rose a wispy trail of greyish white smoke.

The tree line disappeared behind them as the troika passed into the clearing and into view came a modest traditional Russian izba. Made from logs and clay, it sat inside a yard, which also enclosed a vegetable garden, hay shed, and barn all within a simple woven stick fence.

Vitaly, looking to his right and slightly behind him, noticed a small cemetery enclosed within another woven stick fence, but a distance from the izba and next to the road. As they passed by it, he made out three graves. Upon the closest one, carved into a short plank of wood, was the name Alexei.

"Ah, my daughters," said Feliks enthusiastically, face lighting up as he said it and he began waving to them. Vitaly's attention was immediately drawn to three feminine figures in various locations around the yard. A fourth figure descended the stairs from the doorway of the izba as they turned right, trundling through the gateway into the yard and gently towards the barn.

"Hello, Papa," called the closest girl from the vegetable

garden enthusiastically, turning to wave to her father before placing her hands on her hips and observing the stranger accompanying her father with curiosity. Both men waved back, Vitaly somewhat sheepishly as Feliks drove the troika and cart into the barn. Once inside, Feliks applied the break and jumped to the ground, Vitaly following suit as the women approached, the pain in his leg receding now that he could fully extend it.

The four of them came to a stop in the sunshine outside the open barn door and as their father approached, they broke into bright smiles. One by one they embraced him, sweetly kissing him on the cheek before enquiring as to how his day in the woods had been. They then admired and complimented him on his impressive collection of firewood.

That completed, the four turned to look at Vitaly with a combination of confusion and curiosity before one, whom Vitaly presumed to be the oldest, asked, "Who is the gentleman, Papa?"

Feliks, looking at Vitaly, beamed before replying, "Girls, I would like you to meet our new friend. This is Vitaly. Vitaly, these four lovely young women are my daughters." As he said it, Feliks made a sweeping motion in the direction of the four girls. Meanwhile Vitaly smiled back nervously.

"I'm afraid our new friend here is lost and a little injured as I'm sure you can tell," said Feliks wryly to the crowd. "And in repayment for his assistance earlier, he will be joining us for dinner," he finished to amused looks.

"Okay, Papa," replied the girl again, inspecting Vitaly's profile with concern.

"No doubt you would all like some different company for a change," Feliks continued, very matter of fact, placing his arms behind his back and bouncing on the balls of his feet, "and he will be spending the night, right here in the barn, if he so chooses," he added, beaming at Vitaly. "Otherwise, he would be forced to wander the woods in the dark which as we know, can be treacherous."

"Okay, Papa," replied the four girls, this time in sync, almost as if rehearsed. Vitaly hadn't been listening though; he'd become distracted. The second girl from the left looked familiar. He'd definitely seen her somewhere before and recently. Then it hit him: it was her, the girl from the dream. But how could that be? He'd never met her before. He stared at her transfixed, her large dark blue eyes dancing, eyes that were like saucers.

The Four Daughters

"Does our barn meet your approval, Vitaly?" asked Feliks jovially but Vitaly failed to reply, distracted by the presence of the girl.

"Vitaly?" Feliks asked again. It wasn't the question but the giggles of the girls that brought Vitaly back to the present. He looked at his host and smiled goofily before nodding his head in approval.

"Very well then," Feliks said. "Helga, Tiana, if you wouldn't mind, I explained to our new friend how you are trained nurses and practiced during the war." He smiled proudly. "Vitaly will need some attention before dinner."

The two girls, Helga and Tiana, looked from their father to Vitaly and smiled pleasantly before replying, "Okay, Papa," in unison.

"But where are my manners?" exclaimed Feliks, annoyed with himself. "My apologies Vitaly, introductions are necessary," he finished excitedly.

"This is my oldest, Helga," he said, and the girl closest to him stepped forward and shook Vitaly's hand. She smiled sweetly, masterfully disguising her trepidation.

"Tiana," Feliks added, as Helga stepped back and the girl Vitaly had incorrectly presumed to be the oldest stepped forward and also exchanged pleasantries.

"Marta." This time the mystery girl stepped forward. She stared into Vitaly's eyes flirtatiously and after shaking hands, placed hers behind her back and swivelled her hips hypnotically. From behind her, her sisters giggled in amusement.

"That will do, Marta," said Feliks with exasperation, stepping to her and gently tugging on the back of her dress before she slowly re-joined the line.

"And, my youngest, Anka." Who stepped forward unsmiling and searched Vitaly's face suspiciously.

All four women were attractive, Vitaly thought, although Marta was by far the prettiest. As she stood there smiling, she radiated with both beauty and femininity. He quickly found that his eyes being drawn to her unconsciously.

All four were dressed in basic peasant attire: a combination of plain dark-coloured embroidered sarafans over a white or light coloured rubikha, their hair tied up and covered by a similarly coloured shawl, likely he thought, to protect their pretty faces from the sun and keep their hair neat and clean, which would be challenging in this primitive environment.

"And they are good girls." Feliks beamed proudly, placing his arm around Helga's shoulders. "And they take excellent care of me," he added, to bashful smiles from his daughters.

"Helga here," he squeezed her proudly as she turned scarlet, "is an excellent pianist, although unfortunately we no longer have a piano. Sadly, we had to leave it behind in Petrograd," he stated remorsefully as he looked from one daughter to the next. "They can all cook and sew, read and write and speak fluent Russian, English and French. My late son, he could play the balalaika and..."

"Papa!" the four girls spoke in unison, Helga following with a sharp, "shush." Then, tenderly putting her arm around her father's shoulders, she looked him in the eye and continued in a much softer tone, "Papa, you know it upsets us when you talk about Alexei."

Both Helga and Feliks turned to look at Vitaly, their eyes boring into him before Feliks spoke.

"I'm so sorry, Vitaly," said Feliks, sadly. "I was momentarily lost in a memory."

"It's okay, I understand," replied Vitaly sympathetically. "that's your son," he said, pointing towards Feliks, "and your brother," he added, making a sweeping gesture towards the four girls, "and he passed away. Feliks mentioned him and your mother to me earlier on the ride here."

To this news the girls exchanged nervous glances. Vitaly was confused by their reactions and suddenly felt a little uncomfortable. Was he missing something? Had he said something wrong? Before any more awkwardness could materialise, Vitaly spoke again and followed up with a reassuring smile.

"Yes, they're very beautiful," said Vitaly, his eyes locked on to Maria who he was referring to specifically. "Helga, Tiana, Marta and Anka," he recited slowly, taking his eyes off Marta and moving them from one to the other in turn whilst ticking their names off on his fingers.

"Very good, Vitaly," said Feliks, pleased both at his attentiveness and at the change of subject.

"Papa?" asked Tiana, turning to her father.

"Yes, Tiana?" replied Feliks.

"While we are pleased to meet our guest, my sisters and I still have to finish our chores before we can begin dinner. So, forgive us for being rude," Tiana said, looking at Vitaly, "but we must be excused," she added, with another pleasant smile.

"Of course, girls, of course," replied Feliks, himself smiling and with a nod of understanding. "Vitaly and I will occupy ourselves. Would you mind helping me unload the wood?" he asked Vitaly as the four girls turned to walk away, Marta more slowly than the others as she successfully recaptured Vitaly's gaze.

With reluctance, he pulled his eyes away from her again before replying, "It'd be my pleasure," and offered Feliks a smile, pleased that the awkwardness had passed.

"But wait, girls," Feliks remarked. "What about looking over Vitaly's injuries?" and all four turned back to look at their father and Vitaly again before Helga spoke.

"I can see no urgent need as of this moment, Papa," she stated dismissively, Tiana nodding in agreement beside her. However, they both stepped forwards and began inspecting him regardless. They both smiled at him sweetly before Helga inspected the bruise on his temple and Tiana took hold of his forearm and inspected his bloodied elbow.

"This will need sutures," exclaimed Tiana, meeting Vitaly's eyes.

"And how does your head feel?" asked Helga with concern.

"It's fine now, thank you," replied Vitaly self-consciously as Feliks, Marta and Anka watched on from nearby.

"And how was it earlier?" asked Helga with a sharp look.

"You had what? Blurred vision and dizziness didn't you, Vitaly?" interjected Feliks, drawing everyone's attention. All of them quickly looked back to Vitaly as he simply nodded.

"And now?" Helga asked firmly. Her eyes boring into his and making him feel surprisingly nervous.

"Nothing but a slight headache," he replied, continuing to meet her gaze.

"Okay then," she replied, turning to her father. "Unload the wood and when you come inside, I'll take a closer look," she explained. "I'm not particularly concerned. How about you, Tiana?" she asked her sister.

"I think if he was in any danger, it's likely passed by now," Tiana replied while inspecting Vitaly's temple herself. He flinched as she gently brushed his hair away but quickly found that he enjoyed her soft touch on his skin.

"Did you vomit?" she asked, again meeting his eye.

"No," replied Vitaly.

"Did you feel nauseous?" she asked.

"Yes."

"But you didn't vomit?"

"No."

"Do you remember losing consciousness?" she asked, as his expression changed to one of confusion. Carefully, he thought about his answer before replying.

"If I did, which I didn't, I don't remember," he stated confidently.

"Okay," she replied, but her eyes continued to search his face uncertainly. A few seconds later however, now satisfied with his answers, she flashed him another friendly smile and in unison with Tiana, turned back to her father.

"So, are you satisfied girls?" asked Feliks seriously.

"I think so," she said sweetly. "All of us can keep an eye on him over dinner but I'm confident he'll be okay," she finished with a nod to Helga.

"And we can suture your elbow after dinner," added Helga, turning to look at Vitaly and nodding her head.

"Excellent then." Feliks clapped with delight. "Careful not to bang that," he added to Vitaly, pointing at his injured elbow as the party began to disperse. Helga turned and walked away towards the izba. Tiana, with bucket in hand, headed towards the river and the other two girls, the vegetable garden. Disappointed, Vitaly watched Marta as she walked away.

As if sensing his gaze, she untied her shawl. Beautiful long dark brown hair fell down over her shoulders and back. Wow, that's definitely her, he thought, struggling to look away as she playfully retied it, all the while not daring to look back in his direction.

"Ah, Vitaly?" asked Feliks, tapping him on the shoulder to get his attention.

Regaining his senses, Vitaly quickly turned his attention to Feliks. "I'm sorry," he said, shaking his head apologetically.

"No need to be," Feliks chuckled in reply. "You're not the first man to fall under my daughter's spell. But be warned," and he suddenly became very serious, "they're all arranged."

Vitaly looked back at his host with a combination of shock and disappointment before, in response to his expression, Feliks broke out in laughter.

"They're not really, Vitaly," he explained with an amused grin.

"Oh, okay then," replied Vitaly, relieved. Not that it mattered, he thought. He was currently on the run from the Bolsheviks. At the moment, a marriage wouldn't exactly be manageable.

"Now, our wood pile is over here," explained Feliks, interrupting Vitaly's thoughts and pointing to a corner of the barn that contained a rather depleted looking pile of neatly stacked firewood.

Vitaly nodded his head in understanding and began helping Feliks to firstly unload the wood and then stack it. Immediately noticing Vitaly's limp, Feliks asked, "And now what's wrong? Your leg?" Pointing at it.

"Injured it fighting the Germans," replied Vitaly quickly

before changing the subject. "How old are your daughters, Feliks?"

"Hmm, let me think," Feliks replied, now standing with an armful of wood. "Helga is twenty-eight, Tiana twenty-six, Marta twenty-four and Anka, twenty-two."

"And none of them are married?" Vitaly asked, cautiously.

"No. no, no. I was just teasing you," replied Feliks. "Nor have they been. After they lost their mother, well, something like that makes you very close," he added. "However, there are two Latvian boys from the village who often visit. I think they have intentions."

"Is that Kyrubol?" asked Vitaly.

"Yes," replied Feliks. "While they provide us with the goods that we can't produce ourselves, they also regularly bring gifts for my daughters and are particularly attentive to Helga and Tiana, often accompanying them on long walks along the river and through the woods."

"And the other two?" asked Vitaly.

"Anka, I don't believe is interested," replied Feliks, shaking his head. "Marta on the other hand has, since she was a young girl, spoken of her desires of marriage and children," he said, looking at Vitaly knowingly. "Sadly though, life thus far has stood in her way," he finished, before neatly stacking his armful of wood onto the increasingly large stack.

They emptied the cart quickly before unhitching the horse and placing him inside his stall where they ensured there was an adequate supply of water and grains. Closing the gate, they then manoeuvred the troika and cart so they rested side by side. They then exited the barn and closed the two heavy wooden doors with the latch clicking securely behind them.

"Cigarette?" asked Feliks. "Or would you perhaps prefer a pipe? I can offer you both," he added, smiling.

"A cigarette will be fine, thank you," replied Vitaly, reaching out and accepting one from Feliks.

Feliks pulled a match from his pocket and lit it. He held it out to Vitaly, lighting his cigarette, then his own. "Ah," he exhaled after taking a long satisfying drag. He leaned against the barn door, eyes shaded by the bill of his cap, and looked over the tops of the trees at the lowering sun. Long shadows now crept over the clearing containing his family's farm. "I love it here," he said with contentment.

"It's beautiful," replied Vitaly, shielding his eyes with his forearm and exhaling cigarette smoke as he spoke. Looking around fervently, he'd lost sight of the alluring Marta, her sisters too.

The two men stood there quietly, cast under the spell of and absorbed by the ambiance of the late afternoon. Minutes passed in slow motion without a single word passing between them. Finally, breaking the spell, Feliks crushed out his cigarette and spoke.

"Well, shall we join the ladies inside, Vitaly? Dinner should almost be ready by now. If not, that merely means there's time for another cigarette or to enjoy a pre-meal vodka," he said enthusiastically.

"That sounds excellent," exclaimed Vitaly. "You best lead the way then, my friend," he added, placing his hand on Feliks' shoulder before off they went with gusto down the driveway and towards the front door.

A Family Dinner

The two men ascended the stairs, Feliks halting at the top to first open and then hold open the door for Vitaly to enter. Muttering his thanks, Vitaly crossed the threshold and came to a stop just inside, observing the room with interest.

He stood inside a very standard and traditional izba, perhaps more modest than most but very similar to his own family's back in Virubol. It was made of thick pine, distinctive by its smell, with river clay used for filling between the logs.

The roof had a steep pitch, designed to efficiently assist with the dissipation of snow which could be considerable in Siberia during the winter. There were several small windows which allowed a limited amount of light to enter but more importantly in winter, would allow less heat to escape and were likely the only source of glass in the entire home.

Central to all of this was the stove. Taking up roughly an eighth of the floor space, it was made of a combination of clay and stone and set off to the right-hand side of the single room dwelling. It was designed to retain heat for long periods of time which was achieved by funnelling the heat through a labyrinth of passages that warmed the stones it was constructed of and thus radiate heat throughout the room.

"Come and sit, Vitaly," said Tiana politely, motioning to him to approach the moderately-sized wooden table in the centre of the room. He made a motion to remove his hat, forgetting he'd misplaced it, and ran his hand through his hair instead before walking towards her. She slid a wooden seat out for him at the head of the table which he gladly took, grateful for the chance to rest his legs. Feliks took the seat at the opposite end.

Marta approached, vodka and water jugs in hand which she placed on the table next to him. Smiling her enchanting smile, she asked, "Vodka, Vitaly? Or water? We also have fresh milk from our cow."

Smiling back and staring into her eyes again, he replied, "Vodka, please."

"Yes, vodka for me too please, Marta," interrupted Feliks.

"Hold on!" interjected Tiana. "Let me take a better look at you first, Vitaly." She stepped towards his chair. "Marta, will you hold the light up to his face please?" She asked, pointing to the kerosene lamp nearby.

Marta picked up the lamp and held it up in front of Vitaly's eyes before looking to her sister for further instruction.

"Move it in nice and close, Marta, I want to see how his pupils react," explained Tiana before taking her sister's arm and guiding it closer to his face. "Vitaly, please lean your head back and close your eyes and then open them when I say," she added, before both obligingly followed her instructions as Feliks watched on curiously. "Okay, you can open them," said Tiana several seconds later.

She looked deeply into Vitaly's eyes, not that he could tell, he was temporarily blinded by the light. However, his vision recovered quickly and must've been satisfactory for Tiana smiled approvingly. "They responded normally," she stated as he blinked the stars from his eyes. "You can put the light back Marta, thank you. And I see no reason why you can't have a vodka now, Vitaly," she finished approvingly.

"Thank you," he replied.

"You're welcome," she replied with a casual smile before she took his arm and examined his elbow again. "Hmm, your elbow, like I explained earlier, will need sutures and a bandage."

"Okay," he nodded in reply.

"I have a needle and some silk thread, I'll just need to boil them first to ensure they're sterile," she explained while noting Vitaly's worried expression. "It's rudimentary I know, but it'll work," she added hastily. "I'll apply these after dinner," she finished, before turning away and walking over to join her sisters by the stove.

Meanwhile, Marta produced two glasses which she filled with vodka, pouring generously, Vitaly's first, then her father's, before she placed the bottle down between the two men and again looked at Vitaly to whom she smiled and flashed her eyes flirtatiously.

Catching her father's gaze, she turned crimson before abruptly turning away and re-joining her sisters. Meanwhile, Vitaly had become very interested in his glass of vodka and equally mindful of her father sitting across from him.

Feliks smiled knowingly before saying "Nah-zda-rovh-yeh" and the two men toasted each other in unison, lifting their glasses into the air before knocking back their first delicious mouthfuls.

Vitaly continued to observe his surroundings. He noticed five military cots in the corner, obscured previously by the gigantic stove. Around the cots hung multiple ropes fastened from the izba's supporting pine beams. From these ropes hung sheets, used as privacy curtains he assumed, much like in his own home.

There was minimal furniture: this dining table, several chairs and an old wooden couch with a worn mattress covered in a patchwork quilt that rested under one of the windows. Beside it was a balalaika. Feliks noticed him looking at it. "That belonged to my son," he said with a sad smile.

Behind the door against the wall rested a Mosin-Nagant rifle and from a rung on the coat rack above hung a Nagant pistol inside a leather holster. Vitaly also possessed both weapons which were distinctive of the Imperial Russian Army. Spotting the rifle, Vitaly was reminded that his and his bag were still under the troika's seat in the barn.

"I left my rifle and bag in your troika," he told Feliks, concerned.

Looking at him with amusement, Feliks responded, "No matter, they'll be there when you go to bed. Just remember to take them with you in the morning. I'll drive you back to the clearing and you can make a start from there."

"Thank you, that's very kind," replied Vitaly with an appreciative smile.

"You're welcome," replied Feliks. "I imagine the girls will want to send you off with something to eat. I wouldn't dare to try and leave here without whatever it is, or you'll never be welcomed back," he added with a laugh, which Vitaly returned.

Vitaly continued to look around the room. There were ample cooking utensils and upon the stove were several pots of varying sizes boiling away under the watchful eyes of the sisters. Whatever it was they were cooking smelled delicious and Vitaly's stomach growled.

"Not long now, Papa," said Anka as she moved past the table. She was barely audible over the sounds of boiling water and the chattering of her sisters. Vitaly watched as she stopped by some shelves and removed several wooden plates. She placed these down in front of him before returning with a handful of silver cutlery.

"What are we having this evening, Anka?" Feliks asked his youngest daughter, after swallowing a mouthful of vodka and gently taking hold of her wrist as she passed by him.

She stopped and turned to face him. "Solyanka, Veal Orloff, Kurnik and some Borodinsky bread," she said before turning to Vitaly and offering him a forced smile. Satisfied, her father relinquished his grip and she walked away.

"I don't think she likes me very much," Vitaly told Feliks, amused.

"She distrusts strangers, my friend, which makes her your harshest critic, that is all," replied Feliks reassuringly. "By the night's end she will have warmed up to you," he added. "Are you satisfied with this evening's menu?"

"Yes, very, thank you," replied Vitaly, nodding approvingly. "It all sounds delicious," he added, as his stomach growled again, this time more loudly than before.

"They are good cooks, particularly Helga and Tiana," said Feliks proudly. "If the Latvian boys were smart, they'd have proposed years ago. Although I'm not sure they'd leave here; it would be good for them to get away, start a family and so forth," he added, locking eyes with Vitaly.

"How long did you say you've lived here?" asked Vitaly.

"We came here late July, early August 1918," replied Feliks, stroking his chin thoughtfully.

"And where did you move from? Mogilev?" asked Vitaly curiously.

"No, no, no. I was only based in Mogilev during the war," stated Feliks. "My home, that is, our home," he stated, waving towards his daughters, "was in Petrograd. Then from there we travelled to Tobolsk and on to here via Ekaterinburg," he added. "I intended to keep my family safe and stay in front of and as far away from the revolution as possible." He smiled resignedly. "As a monarchist, Ekaterinburg was a bad decision."

"Papa," interrupted Helga, catching her father's attention. "Dinner is ready." Which propelled the four women into action. They began placing down separate bowls of steaming hot food onto the table right in front of the two men before sitting themselves down. While not a copious amount of food, it would ensure the six of them would not go hungry, thought Vitaly.

"Would you join us in prayer, Vitaly?" asked Feliks tentatively.

Vitaly met his eye and looked back, unsure. "I must confess, I haven't prayed in some time," he responded.

"Not to worry, my friend," replied Feliks with amusement. "Take a hand and we'll do the rest." And he did, joining the family in prayer.

Once completed they helped themselves to the dishes and dug into their meal. For several minutes there was silence, broken only by the clattering of cutlery and the sounds of breathing, chewing and swallowing.

"I believe, or at least I've heard rumours that Ekaterinburg is where the Bolsheviks executed the Czar," stated Vitaly, tactlessly breaking the silence after swallowing a mouthful of solyanka.

"Yes, I believe so too," replied Feliks after an uncomfortable pause. He followed that affirmation by downing his glass of vodka. "We would have been in the city at around the same time I believe," he added reluctantly before pouring himself another glass. He offered the bottle to Vitaly, who shook his head.

"No thank you," said Vitaly, holding up his hand. "You knew the Czar?" he asked. In response, the four women exchanged nervous glances between themselves and then their father, who after clearing his throat, replied.

"Yes, although not well," he said nervously, returning the gazes of his daughters.

"What was he like?" asked Vitaly. "Or at least, what was your impression of him?" and he sat back in his chair eagerly awaiting Feliks' reply.

Feliks, stalling, again drained his glass of vodka before slowly refilling it. Vitaly could sense his unease at the question and wondered why he was being so cagey. Vitaly, looking from one daughter to the next, could see the same look on their faces as their father. Turning back to Feliks, the two men locked eyes.

"He had a good heart," said Feliks. "To those who knew or met him that was clear. He loved Russia and wanted a unified Russia. He'd be horrified by the Civil War. Russians fighting Russians!" Feliks shook his head in disgust. "He has been described as indecisive, which personally I blame on the many ministers in his cabinet providing him with confusing and conflicting information."

He continued, "He was however a doting father and loving husband who understandably was more concerned about the ailing health of his haemophiliac son than the trials and tribulations of the Russian Empire over which he ruled."

Vitaly sat even further back in his chair, stunned at this revelation. "His son suffered from haemophilia?" By this time everyone was staring at Feliks transfixed, his daughters looking almost frightened.

"Uh, yes," replied Feliks, catching himself. "I believe so, although I doubt there are many people who know that," he added before looking around nervously at his daughters.

"I've never heard that," stated Vitaly earnestly, looking around the table for confirmation which did not come.

"Yes, like I said, few would," replied Feliks softly. "One thing I always noticed about the Czar and the entire family for that matter was, they were visible. Their son, the Czarevich Alexei, was not, although he did accompany his father to Mogilev which is where I met him."

"Wow!" said Vitaly. "That's incredible! How tragic for the Czar and his family. Perhaps that helps explain the rationale for his abdication, also Grigori Rasputin's presence in their lives? He was reputed to be a healer after all," he added.

"That is my impression. Replied Feliks. I, um, heard them talking about an incident in Spala, just before the war if I recall correctly. That's in Poland. The family owned a hunting lodge there. The child injured himself playing and suffered a massive bleed that threatened his life. Through faith and prayer, Rasputin was able to heal the boy despite being more than three thousand kilometres away."

"Incredible!" said Vitaly in awe. "It makes me think, what if the Romanovs had released this information to the public? The Czarevich being ill and Rasputin being his healer or doctor. Perhaps they'd still sit on the Imperial throne?"

"Perhaps," replied Feliks. "The problem remains though; the boy was sick. Haemophilia was passed down the female line from Queen Victoria to her granddaughter, the Czarina Alexandra, and onto the Czarevich. It affects males. Of the several different male descendants of Victoria who suffered from it, none lived to adulthood. The Czarina's own brother died from it in infancy."

He continued, "It was therefore unlikely that the boy would have survived regardless of Rasputin's supposed skills or powers. In fact, I think the so-called mad monk should be praised for his achievement in keeping the Czarevich alive and healthy for as long he did. Regardless though, the Empire would've been left without an heir," he finished, before tossing back another mouthful of vodka.

"What about Grand Duke Michael?" asked Vitaly, impressed with Feliks' knowledge on the subject and not wanting the discussion to end.

"Let's finish our meals first, hey Vitaly? They're getting cold," stated Feliks firmly but pleasantly, changing the subject and leaning forward over his plate and scooping up a spoon full of solyanka.

Crestfallen, Vitaly managed an understanding smile before replying, "Sure." As he said it, he looked from Feliks to his daughters in acknowledgment. Marta smiled back like a Cheshire cat. "You know, you actually look a lot like him. The Czar," said Vitaly through a mouthful of solyanka-soaked bread. "Grow out your beard and you could claim the throne!" he joked, chuckling good naturedly in an attempt to lighten the atmosphere.

At this, Feliks stared back at Vitaly without smiling, which made Vitaly uncomfortable. Obviously, he'd done it again and said the wrong thing. They held each other's gaze for several more increasingly uncomfortable seconds before Feliks finally broke. Turning his attention to his daughters, he asked, "Well girls, what do you think?"

They looked around at each other nervously before Helga asked timidly, "Think about what, Papa?"

"About becoming Grand Duchesses?" he asked very seriously. Holding their gaze, he finally cracked and broke into a broad smile, causing everyone to laugh, although the four women, excluding Marta that is, were somewhat reserved.

"It's settled then," said Feliks and he banged his balled-up fist on the table with mock enthusiasm, startling Marta, who was seated next to him. "Tomorrow, we leave for Moscow to tell the Bolsheviks that we're retaking the throne," he added, laughing.

"Take, not retake, Papa," corrected Tiana, laughing along with her father.

Vitaly laughed along too, nonplussed but pleased at the change in atmosphere. Everyone then returned to their meals, the izba quickly refilling with the familiar sounds of mealtime in the presence of good company.

Wife, Mother and Son

"I apologise if I crossed a line earlier," said Vitaly about an hour later as the two men descended the front stairs. He examined his sutured and bandaged elbow and flexed the joint confidently.

"No, no, it's okay, Vitaly. I defend the Czar because I feel he gets criticised harshly, not that you were critical. Most people don't know of and certainly wouldn't understand the struggles he faced," replied Feliks reassuringly.

"Tiana did a good job on this," stated Vitaly with pleasure, referring to his elbow. "The vodka stinged, the needle going in and out too, but thankfully, it's all over now." He smiled pleasantly.

"Tiana and Helga both excelled at nursing," Feliks replied proudly. "It was a proud day for our family when they joined their mother at the Red Cross. They were very popular with the soldiers and I think they saw it as their duty."

"Well, it shows," replied Vitaly. "Their skill, that is," he added, inspecting his elbow once again. "Another thing," he continued, "and I mean no offence, but I suspect you're not being entirely honest with me," He finished carefully, relieved as Feliks chuckled in response.

The two men turned left at the bottom of the stairs and right out onto the gravel driveway before pausing to light their cigarettes. "Do you care to elaborate as to how, my friend?" He asked pleasantly, lighting Vitaly's then his own before waving the match out.

"Certainly," replied Vitaly as they turned and resumed their journey, the sound of crunching gravel beneath their feet. "How is it you know so much about the Czar, Czarina, Rasputin, Queen Victoria and haemophilia? It's impressive to say the least considering you only met him, what did you say? Twice?"

With Feliks leading the way they left the driveway, turning left onto the road, Vitaly alongside but a half step behind. They stepped of the gravel into the field, their crunching footsteps now muffled by the soft grass. Vitaly suspected they were heading towards the small cemetery on the edge of the woods.

"Living in a metropolis the size of Petrograd has similarities to living in a village like Virubol, Vitaly," replied Feliks, exhaling a mouthful of smoke.

"How so?" asked Vitaly curiously before a long drag on his own cigarette.

"You hear things. Rumours, stories, scandals and so forth," replied Feliks. "I must ask, how is it you know what haemophilia is? That knowledge surprises me. In fact, to be completely honest, there have been several things about you that have surprised me."

"Really?" asked Vitaly in reply. "Like what exactly?" he asked with an unintentional sharpness. To soften the blow, he asked again but with more reserve. "What about me has surprised you?"

"I'm curious how a boy from such a rural village like

Virubol is so obviously educated," he finished, smiling at his friend.

"My mother was the village school teacher," replied Vitaly, amused.

"So, you're the son of a farmer and school teacher?" asked Feliks, more to himself than Vitaly as he scratched his chin in thought. "I'd like to hear more about them," he added.

"Hmm, that's interesting," replied Vitaly thoughtfully as they continued across the field.

"My curiosity about your parents?" asked Feliks, confused.

"No, not that. I was thinking more in regards to what you said before, about the similarities of Petrograd and Virubol," replied Vitaly. "Should I disregard what you told me over dinner? Was it merely rumours, stories and scandal?" He looked at Feliks, struggling to keep the sarcasm from his voice. He was enjoying the repartee.

"They are not rumours," replied Feliks firmly. "I spent much of my life in Petrograd, much in the way you spent much of your life in Virubol, I suspect. I come from a family that was fortunate enough in its means to afford me an education and even to travel. I imagine the first time you left your village, that is for more than a night or two, was when you joined the Imperial Army?"

"That's correct," replied Vitaly, curious as to where this conversation was heading. Dark shadows cast by the trees now stretched out across the field obscuring the cemetery from the setting sun. Vitaly could just make out the three grave markers and remembered Feliks' son Alexei lay closest to the road.

"Would I be correct in presuming you know everyone in your village?" asked Feliks.

"Correct. Or almost correct. There are around two hundred of them," replied Vitaly.

"Obviously, I don't know everyone in Petrograd, but I

would estimate that I know as many people as you know in Virubol. Some influential people included, and more than one who in some capacity was required to frequent one or more of the Imperial Palaces."

"Now I understand," replied Vitaly with clarity. "These sources are reliable and without doubt discreet?"

"That is correct," replied Feliks. "There is so much mystery surrounding the Romanovs. So much rumour and intrigue. One must be careful when wading through it. I can assure you the information I shared with you is factually correct."

"And who was your source?" asked Vitaly boldly.

"I would never betray a friend, least of all one that has since passed," Feliks replied remorsefully. "And I would hope that new friends would respect that," he added, turning his head and offering Vitaly a smile before briefly pausing to crush out his cigarette.

"Of course. Again, I'm sorry if I touched a nerve," said Vitaly apologetically as the two men recommenced walking, now side by side and crossed into the shadows. "I don't know the Czar and having never met him I'm in no position to judge him." He looked again at Feliks, this time for reassurance. Upon receiving no response, he added. "I know what you must be thinking. I joined the Bolsheviks and therefore I must be a rabid antimonarchist. For the record I am not. I stated back in the woods that I disliked their methods and I stand by that statement."

"Why would you join and then abandon the revolution so quickly?" asked Feliks, his confusion evident by his tone.

Both men suddenly stopped walking and turned to face each other. Vitaly dropped his cigarette to the ground and aggressively crushed it out beneath his foot before reaching out and grabbing Feliks arm. Although the twilight obscured his face, Feliks knew Vitaly was annoyed at the question, one which unbeknownst to Feliks, he'd been asked several times before.

"Let me make it very clear," Vitaly replied passionately. "I love Russia and make no apologies for that but could it be better? Yes! My grandfather, my father's father, was a serf, something that Alexander II abolished. Now, despite being able to own his own farm, my father still has to work his fingers to the bone to merely scratch a living which is made all the worse by the Bolsheviks' requisitions."

"I thought that had stopped with the end of the war?" replied Feliks with alarm.

"Not around here it hasn't, replied Vitaly passionately. "All the stress and strain has left him somewhat broken and he relies heavily upon me to help, which before the war I was, albeit unwilling, able to do. I saw a different future for myself and jumped at the opportunity to escape the farm, village and Siberia, so I lied about my age and joined the Imperial Army. I've no regrets."

In response, their eyes met, and one studied the other. Feliks took hold of Vitaly's wrist and gently removed his hand from his forearm then patiently waited in silence as Vitaly's breath slowed and returned to normal. Finally sensing it was time, he spoke.

"Perhaps it is I who now owes you an apology, Vitaly," Feliks said with an understanding smile. "That was a careless remark and I meant no offence by it," he added, releasing Vitaly's arm and extending his own for a handshake which was gladly returned.

"Now, I would like you to meet my wife and son," Feliks said, changing the subject.

They had reached the cemetery and stood just outside its boundary. Out of respect, Vitaly hesitantly waited outside as

Feliks stepped through the small gateway and came to a stop in front of the middle grave.

Feliks looked around at him, then beckoned him to join him inside. "It's okay, Vitaly," he said appreciatively, waving him inside. "Allow me to introduce you to my wife and son, Alexandra and Alexei," he added proudly.

Vitaly looked down and read the names carved into the planks of wood tied to the crosses. Alexandra rested in the middle, Alexei on her right and closest to the fence and road. The grave to the left of Alexandra was different though, thought Vitaly. The name on it read George.

"George? Who is George?" he asked Feliks casually.

"George was an elderly man who passed by here one night around five years ago," replied Feliks vaguely, clearly focusing his attention on the graves of his wife and son. "I'd hoped to have headstones for these two by now," he added sadly.

"May I ask what happened?" asked Vitaly reluctantly, to which he received no reply. Perhaps he didn't hear me, he thought, so sheepishly he asked again, but Feliks continued to ignore him. He tapped him on the shoulder, which finally drew Feliks' attention.

"I'm sorry, what?" asked Feliks, a little dazed and turning to look at Vitaly.

"What happened to George?" Vitaly asked again.

"Oh yes, well, he knocked on our door one night. He was out walking and it had started raining. I don't know where he was heading or where he had come from. It was late so we offered him some food and a bed in the barn for the night, much like yourself. Anka found him the next morning, he'd passed in his sleep."

"Is that why she doesn't like strangers?" asked Vitaly with a wry smile.

Feliks chuckled. "I doubt it. When you live in the country

you see death everywhere. Cows, sheep, horses, chickens. Wild animals are always turning up too. So no, however, it was, as I'm sure you could understand, a bit of a shock. One of the few facts he divulged was that he had no family so we decided to bury him here."

"That's kind of you," said Vitaly. "And your wife and son? What happened to them? If you don't mind me asking?"

"My wife had heart troubles, a condition our son sadly inherited," Feliks replied. "Unlike her, he'd suffered on and off from within a few weeks of his birth until he passed away at only fifteen, in 1919. She followed two months afterwards, his death being the catalyst I believe," he finished before turning back to their graves and wiping away a tear.

"I'm sorry for your loss," said Vitaly, bringing his hand up to rest on Feliks' shoulder tenderly. "I'm not married nor do I have children so I couldn't begin to understand what that's like. You're lucky though," he added, before Feliks turned to look at him again.

"Lucky?" Feliks asked, a little confused.

"Yes, lucky, Feliks, and I just met the four reasons why." Vitaly beamed at him.

Feliks broke into a wide smile. "Thank you," he said, then turned away to wipe away another tear before pulling a handkerchief from his pocket and dabbing it at his nose.

They remained standing there in silence as day slowly turned to night and the darkness overwhelmed the eggplant-coloured sky. Light now shone through the izba's windows, flickering occasionally when a curious face blocked its path. Finally, Feliks offered his wife and son a prayer and Vitaly joined him. Crossing themselves, they turned to each other. Vitaly was the first to speak.

"Thank you for introducing me to your family," he said.

"You're welcome, my friend," replied Feliks affectionately

before he glanced one last time at his wife's grave. "She was my sunshine and he my little sailor," he said softly. "Goodness, it's growing late," he said as he stood on the edge of the moonlit clearing and looked up into the sky. "Could I interest you in a coffee and another cigarette before turning in? I know you have a long walk ahead of you tomorrow."

"Certainly," replied Vitaly with enthusiasm.

"Follow me back to the izba then and we shall see what mischief my daughters are up to," said Feliks before the two men began their walk.

The return trip was completed quickly and within ten minutes the two men lazed comfortably at the bottom of the front stairs on two wooden chairs. Helga brought them each a steaming cup of coffee and they both lit a cigarette before turning their gazes up to the moonlit sky.

"So, your mother is a school teacher?" asked Feliks. "And where did she receive her education?"

"She originally came from Petrograd," replied Vitaly.

"Really? And what is her name?" asked Feliks.

"Yes. She and my father met in Virubol when her family visited the village. Their names are Pyotr and Lena Borisov. My mother's family possessed land there and somehow my father came to work on it at some point. They met and fell in love, much to the disappointment and disapproval of my mother's parents, that is."

"They disapproved? Why?" asked Feliks.

"Because my father was a peasant and they were wealthy, or at least they thought they were. I've no idea really besides what my parents told me, which is very little. I've never met my mother's parents and can't say I really want to. They belong to the bourgeoisie and I suspect my parents hate them."

"How sad," said Feliks, looking Vitaly in the eye. Holding his gaze, they both slowly sipped on their coffee before drawing again on their cigarettes. "Changing the subject, why did you join the Bolsheviks? You didn't explain your reasoning."

"The army was collapsing and men were needlessly dying. I was injured, quite badly actually. I nearly lost this leg," he pointed to his extended right leg before deciding to pull up his trouser leg and show Feliks his scar. Recoiling slightly, Feliks let out a low "My god" before taking another long drag on his cigarette and continuing to stare at the wound with both disgust and amazement.

"And another comrade," explained Vitaly very seriously, his eyes becoming glassy, "a childhood friend of mine from Virubol, who accompanied me when I ran away and joined the army, was killed by the same shell that did this. I saw him literally explode in front of me, showering me in his blood, brain and guts." Looking even more repulsed now, Feliks hand shook as he took another puff on his cigarette.

"Very unpleasant," said Vitaly, shaking his head. "You know, I can still see his face," he added.

"What was his name?" asked Feliks shakily.

"Evgeny. Evgeny Borisov," replied Vitaly softly.

"Borisov? As in your brother?" asked Feliks with concern. Evidently, he had made the connection.

"No," replied Vitaly, voice breaking. "My cousin." Eyes ablaze and boring into Feliks'. Feliks, unresponsive, didn't look away.

"He, ah, he followed me," continued Vitaly. "All because I'd called him a coward if he didn't. It's my fault he's dead."

"How old was he?" asked Feliks.

"Let's see, it's currently late July 1923. So, he would've been seventeen at the time."

"And how old were you?" asked Feliks.

"I had just turned eighteen."

"It's sad, the death of so many young men," replied Feliks thoughtfully. "But blaming yourself for his death is foolish. Being underage, he shouldn't have been there. But, had he not followed you, it's likely he would've volunteered regardless once he did come of age."

"That's all well and true, Feliks, but it doesn't stop this feeling of guilt," retorted Vitaly sharply, holding Feliks' eye.

"No, I understand," he replied, nodding in agreement. "But that's different."

"How?" asked Vitaly.

"What you're referring to is what I believe they call survivor's guilt," replied Feliks.

"And what is that, exactly?" Vitaly inquired.

"That you survived and he didn't," explained Feliks, "and that, despite standing, what, only a few feet apart and being hit by the same shell blast that eviscerated him and only injured you? Here you are a little worse for wear but nonetheless alive," he finished with a kind and understanding smile.

Vitaly looked at his new friend thoughtfully and became immersed in those kind greyish-blue eyes twinkling back at him. For the first time he gave the subject some serious thought. He knew that Evgeny had been too smart to be baited into running away. He had wanted to join the Imperial army and fight, just as Feliks had pointed out and would've joined at the first opportunity regardless.

Perhaps, also for the first time, Vitaly could finally make sense of his feelings regarding his cousin's demise and rationalise them. What was the difference between this stranger telling him this and his family? Well, Feliks had been there. Maybe not literally at the front, but he would've seen and heard things too, which was more than his family had done.

"I know you're right," came Vitaly softly. "My parents and aunt and uncle have expressed similar opinions on the matter. Although I've never admitted to them the specific details of his death."

"Why? They obviously can't blame you any more than I would," Feliks stated firmly.

"Guilt, Feliks, guilt!" replied Vitaly. "I can barely bring myself to look uncle Anatoly and aunt Irina in the eye let alone explain in detail what happened!"

"That doesn't matter though, Vitaly," replied Feliks softly. "Tell me, are you an only child?"

"Yes."

"And was your cousin an only child?"

"No, he has a younger sister."

"Okay, but you're the only two boys in the family?"

"Yes," replied Vitaly, furrowing his brows in confusion as to what this had to do with anything.

"Then would you say, being close in age and growing up in the same village that you were close?"

"We were literally neighbours," replied Vitaly. "But what has this got to do with anything?"

"Everything, my friend!" replied Feliks, himself becoming impassioned. "You were cousins who were probably more like brothers so do you not think that your aunt and uncle would find some comfort in knowing that you were there when he died?"

"I don't know," replied Vitaly, shrugging his shoulders.

"To Evgeny then," said Feliks with exasperation. He raised his coffee into the air where it met Vitaly's. "Nah-zda-rovh-yeh." They both stated before taking another drink.

"And that's why you joined the Bolsheviks?" asked Feliks thoughtfully.

"Yes. And then the Czar abdicated and Kerensky took

control of the government and everything looked positive. Then of course only months later Lenin completed his coup and ousted Kerensky with the aid of the Germans and betrayed us all by surrendering all that territory to our enemies at Brest-Litovsk," replied Vitaly.

"In what battle were you were injured?" asked Feliks.

"At the close of the Brusilov offensive outside of Kowel in Galicia," replied Vitaly.

"Ah yes, the effective end of Russia as an active participant in the war," replied Feliks with dejection.

"You remember it too?" asked Vitaly, Feliks nodding in confirmation

"It's hard to forget," replied Feliks bitterly. "One point seven million Russians deployed, approximately one million killed, give or take. Alexei Brusilov was very successful but was only a small part of the overall offensive, which was a dismal failure."

Vitaly nodded his head in agreement and was moved by the evident emotion shown on Feliks' face at the recollection of such a considerable number of men lost.

"You would've fought under Alexei Evert?" asked Feliks.

"That's correct," replied Vitaly, impressed, but Feliks shook his head disapprovingly.

"He was a weak link," he said bitterly but didn't care to elaborate.

"I was also involved in the border clash at Mamornita on the Prut River when we crossed into Romania and overwhelmed a detachment of their border guard in the pursuit of the Austria-Hungarian army," Vitaly offered.

"Yes, I remember that too. It caused quite a stir with the Romanians," replied Feliks with a wry smile.

Vitaly took a deep breath then began. "So, my story started out with me wanting a better life and some adventure, then turned into a horrifying experience mixed with pain and suffering, followed by what appeared to be on the surface a positive change, then the expectation and hope of that change before ultimate betrayal," he finished, emitting a loud sigh. "I think people have been writing stories like that for centuries."

Vitaly crushed out his cigarette and tipped out the dregs of his coffee. "It's late and I'm tired with a long walk ahead of me in the morning," he said abruptly. "So, if you wouldn't mind, I'll be off to bed."

"I understand." Feliks smiled. "Are you okay to see yourself to the barn?"

"Yes, I'll be fine. Thank you," replied Vitaly.

"I appreciate you sharing your experience with me tonight, Vitaly," stated Feliks. "As hard as that might have been."

"Thank you for listening, Feliks," replied Vitaly with an appreciative smile. "I think our discussion has helped."

"I hope so my friend," replied Feliks, beaming. They both rose from their seats and shook hands and wished the other a pleasant evening before turning away, Feliks for the front steps and izba, Vitaly for the gravel driveway and barn.

Vitaly had only taken a few steps before he turned and yelled, "Would you thank your daughters for their delicious cooking and bid them a good evening from me, please?" Then a woman's face appeared in the nearest window. It was Marta. He waved to her and she back to him, longingly.

"With pleasure," yelled back Feliks, now obscured by the izba. Satisfied, Vitaly turned and continued onwards towards the barn.

Midnight
Rendezvous

Vitaly slowly entered before pulling the door closed behind him and listening for the latch to click. The barn was illuminated by the moonlight seeping in through several cracks and two open windows. Looking to his left he noticed a lantern hanging from a hook, partly obscured by a pitchfork hanging next to it.

Ignoring the lantern, he removed the pitchfork from its hook. He then began walking slowly across the barn, with care initially, then more confidently as his eyes adjusted to the light.

He manoeuvred around the troika and cart, collecting his bag but leaving the rifle where it was as he wouldn't be needing it. He then stopped at the stall containing the Vyatka horse. There he sat pitchfork and bag down against one of the barn's pine roof supports. Resting his arms on top of the gate, he leaned down and observed the sleeping horse, watching as its solid torso rose and fell with each breath as it snored rhythmically.

For several minutes he simply stood there enjoying the

ambiance of the warm night. The wooden shutters would be staying open, he thought, not that there was much of a breeze. Looking out the nearest window, he could see the family's cow grazing in the field beyond.

He straightened up, stretching his arms out above him and emitting a loud yawn before picking up the pitchfork and bag and making his way over to the corner stall. Within was a sizeable stack of fresh and comfortable-looking hay. He unlatched the gate and slowly swung it open, securing it and then stepping inside.

Finding a hook, he hung his bag from it then began spreading the stack of hay around using the pitchfork, levelling the centre out into a Vitaly-sized patch to sleep on. Once satisfied, he leaned the pitchfork against a wall and closed the gate behind him.

Turning around, he threw himself backwards, childlike, arms wide, into the soft pile. Upon landing, he sank down several centimetres and made himself comfortable before sleep came upon him quickly.

He was dreaming again, evident from the fuzzy edges of his vision and being thrust back into the hellish nightmare of wartime. However, this time it was different. He was in the woods and there were innumerable soldiers racing around him. Then, from nowhere, Evgeny appeared before him having stepped out from behind the closest tree. He was fastening the front of his trousers when he looked up and spoke.

"If Avekdeev keeps feeding me that stuff he calls coffee, I'll have every tree in this forest watered before the war's over," he said with a laugh.

Vitaly couldn't believe his eyes.

"Vee, what do you reckon?" he asked Vitaly jokingly. "Vee?" he asked again whilst fruitlessly suppressing a grin. But Vitaly couldn't speak so Evgeny continued.

"You must have an iron bladder comrade, or some sort of serious yet possibly beneficial malfunction somewhere down in there," he said with amusement as he pointed to Vitaly's stomach. "Either way, whoever's running this show should take you in for testing. We'd be a much more efficient army if we didn't need to piss every few hours." He laughed again.

"Evgeny!" muttered Vitaly, still struggling to speak.

"What? You agree, don't you?" asked Evgeny accusingly. "That'd be just like you though wouldn't it," he added with a laugh. "Don't let the Boches catch you, they mightn't be as gentle testing the pipes."

"Evgeny?" asked Vitaly again.

"Yeah, Vee?"

"What... where are we?" Vitaly asked, looking around the forest then back to his cousin.

"Just a suggestion, but maybe try drinking more coffee and less vodka in the future," replied Evgeny sarcastically. Vitaly couldn't help but laugh, the feeling of elation finally washing over him at the sight of his cousin.

"You're going to wander off in a drunken stupor one day and accidentally walk in on the Kaiser taking a shit," he continued, bending his arm at the elbow to replicate the Kaisers deformity. "Can you imagine trying to wipe your ass with that bitty arm he's got?" He barely managed to ask before they both roared with laughter.

Then, composing himself, Evgeny suddenly became very serious. "No, no, seriously now, we're in Galicia and everybody's freaking out because the Czar is coming to visit," explained Evgeny and he reached out and pointed over Vitaly's shoulder. "In fact, judging by the looks of that entourage, this is him coming through the trees now."

Vitaly turned to look and found himself confronted by a

collection of well-dressed, clean-uniformed and medal-adorned men.

"What do reckon, Vee?" asked Evgeny from behind. "Never thought we'd see let alone meet the Czar. Suppose he's here to lift morale. I know of several men who've deserted in the last week alone."

But Vitaly wasn't really listening. His focus had been drawn to the man standing at the centre of the group. His face was half obscured, his head being turned away as he spoke with one of Vitaly's comrades. Despite the obstruction Vitaly instinctively knew it was the Czar, his Imperial Highness alive and in the flesh. He was middle aged, of a slight build, short and wore a bushy brown moustache and beard. Vitaly could hear his voice and found it familiar. He could also make out a thin scar running down the right side of his forehead.

"I need you to pay attention, Vee," stated Evgeny from behind before he grabbed his shoulder and pulled him around to face him. The Czar had turned at the same time but was left to stare at the back of Vitaly's head in the distance.

"What is it, Evgeny?" asked Vitaly with frustration. "I was just about to get a look at him!" he added before looking back over his shoulder. He found the Czar had once again turned his head away and was now immersed in another conversation, this time with a different comrade.

"I need you to pay attention," repeated Evgeny. "Which requires you to listen carefully," he added as Vitaly turned back to look at his cousin. Their eyes met and Evgeny smiled.

"It's not your fault," exclaimed Evgeny firmly while Vitaly stared. "It's not your fault!" he repeated with emphasis, unsure if he'd heard him properly, and he stared back at his older cousin, wide-eyed and imploring.

"What's not my fault?" asked Vitaly. But he knew exactly what Evgeny was referring to.

"That I'm dead," exclaimed Evgeny, matter-of-factly.

"What!" shot back Vitaly.

"You know," replied Evgeny sharply whilst giving his cousin a derisive look. "Stop beating yourself up over something that you couldn't control."

"But, you're dead because of me!" stated Vitaly, his frustration and anger rising.

"No," Evgeny replied, smiling and shaking his head from side to side. His nonchalance wasn't helping. Instead, it fuelled Vitaly's feelings of frustration and general lack of understanding.

"How can you be smiling!?" retorted Vitaly sharply. He could feel the emotion welling up inside him and suddenly found himself fighting back tears.

"No idea, comrade," replied Evgeny with a cheeky smile. "This is your dream. But, if you ask me, standing before you right now should be that blue-eyed beauty from Livadia."

"How do you know about her?" asked Vitaly with surprise. His voice broke as he spoke but the abrupt change of subject and distraction, at least momentarily, had stopped any tears from materializing.

"She and I have things in common," he replied. "As in we're both a part of the same subconscious."

"What the hell are you talking about, Evgeny?" asked Vitaly with frustration.

"Listen, Vee, this is a dream and dreams don't have to make sense," he replied. "Hell, you'll likely not remember this when you wake up anyway so why worry? Now pay attention and listen to me and listen carefully because I cannot stress the importance of the following statement. My. Death. Is. Not. Your. Fault!" he added, carefully emphasising every word.

Vitaly looked at his cousin thoughtfully and began shaking

his head in disagreement. He was about to respond but Evgeny cut him off.

"I love you brother, unconditionally! Always have, always will. But now it's time to go." And he smiled again.

"Wait! What!?" replied Vitaly desperately as Evgeny disappeared before him and the dream quickly collapsed into darkness.

He'd been asleep, for how long exactly he was unsure. He stirred and was woken by the sound of the latch clicking on the barn door. He opened his eyes, turned his head to the side, then peered through one of the gaps in the stall's wooden fence.

Instinctively, he longed for his rifle, which being several feet away and through a closed gate was completely useless to him now. He immediately regretted his decision to leave it under the troika's seat.

However, through the moonlit barn two small feet came into view. They were protruding from beneath an ankle-length skirt, its colour indiscernible in the gloom. Relieved, he sat up and instinctively knew who it would be.

"Vitaly," called out Marta softly.

Yes, it was her, he thought joyously, heart skipping a beat. Although, to make sure it was real and avoid a repetition of that morning's disappointment, he pinched himself.

"Vitaly," she called again more loudly.

"I'm over here," he replied, sitting up and resting his elbows on his knees.

"Over where?"

"In the last stall," he answered, unable to help smiling to himself in the darkness.

He listened intently and could just make out her soft muffled steps on the hay-strewn floor. Hearing her stumble and gasp, he called to her again. "Are you okay? Marta?"

"I'm okay. I just tripped. I think I've bruised my ankle," she added with annoyance.

Vitaly stood up to find himself face to face with the beautiful Marta, her eyes reflecting the moonlight filling the room. Her face lit up when she saw him and he could have sworn the room grew brighter when she smiled. She rested her hands on the gate gently, Vitaly mimicking her so that their faces were only millimetres apart.

"Did I wake you?" she asked tentatively.

"Well, yes, but it's okay, Marta," he replied playfully.

"Oh, I'm sorry Vitaly," she said, playing along and touching his arm flirtatiously.

"You came to find me?" he asked, staring into those dark blue eyes.

"Just to check you had everything you needed."

"Just about," he said, grinning sheepishly. "You know, I had a dream about you," he added with reticence, fearful at a negative reaction.

"Oh really?" she replied playfully, her voice rising and filled with curiosity. "And what happened in this dream?" she asked with raised eyebrows.

"I only just remembered where it took place. We were at the Livadia Palace in Crimea. I recognise it now from a photograph I once saw. We were on a balcony at the palace overlooking the Black Sea. We were talking and then we kissed before we laid down on a lounger in each other's arms."

"Then what happened?" she asked, her interest overpowering her confusion.

"Sadly, that's where the dream ended. Your father is to blame," he replied, cheekily.

"Oh," she responded in kind, eyes boring into his soul, which made him feel warm and fuzzy and gave him butterflies.

"That's right," he said. "It was the sound of his axe striking the wood that did it. Most disappointing."

"You were sad that you woke up?" she asked in a whisper, their noses almost touching.

"Very," he replied as his eyes flicked from her eyes to her lips and back again.

Their breaths shortened as their noses touched, then their cheeks, and they gently rubbed their faces together, a loose strand of Marta's hair tickling Vitaly's face.

Emboldened, he pulled away, then taking his hand off the gate he ran the back of his index finger up and along her smooth check and into her hair, brushing the loose strand back over her ear whilst staring into her eyes.

"I'm not going to ask you to...." was all Marta could get out before, using the same hand, Vitaly cupped her face and kissed her passionately. They both closed their eyes, shutting out the world and becoming lost inside the ecstasy with nothing but the wooden gate between them.

When they finally separated, Vitaly ran his hand slowly back down her cheek and under her chin before, using thumb and forefinger, he gently raised her head. Their eyes met, her blue saucers full of anticipation, and upon meeting his, she watched him with intensity. Somehow, it appeared as if her eyes had gotten bigger, he thought.

They kissed several more times before separating again, this time for Vitaly to unlock the stall gate and admit her. Stepping inside, Marta dropped the small pouch she was holding onto a soft pile of straw. Vitaly pulled the gate closed behind her and they turned to face each other and embraced before kissing again. This time even more passionately than before.

They disengaged and both took a step backwards so they would have room to undress. Marta began slowly removing her dress, Vitaly his shirt and pants, the process interrupted only by the overpowering desire and need to embrace and kiss again.

Finally, with Marta's long light-brown hair hanging down over her bare breasts, shoulders and back, they stood there, both naked as the day they were born. They both stood back, admiring each other's naked bodies in the moonlight before embracing again and wildly dragging the other onto the pile of hay. Marta landed on top and Vitaly wrapped his arms around her waist and pulled her in as close to him as possible and the lovemaking began.

Revelations

They lay there entwined. Warm and fuzzy, covered in sweat and wrapped in a blanket Marta had pulled off the railing dividing this stall and the next. She lay on him, her head resting on his chest with her hand gently stroking it. Their breathing had returned to normal although they felt anything but. The oxytocin pulsing through their bodies made sure of that.

Her hair was now messy and strewn about all over the place. It covered Vitaly – not that he minded, he liked how it smelled. He found himself continually kissing her. Between kisses on the lips, he kissed the top of her head, the back of her hand and her forehead. He simply couldn't get enough and neither could she.

They said very little for a long time. They didn't need to. In all their simplicity they enjoyed each other's warm embrace. For Vitaly, the soft smooth silk-like complexion of her skin was the most exotic thing he'd ever experienced. For her, Vitaly's lean yet muscular complexion was the epitome of the rugged masculinity that was desirable in a protector and provider and at this very moment it belonged to her and her alone.

Taking her hand in his he asked, "Are you happy here, Marta?"

She looked up at him. Her saucer eyes were filled with sadness. Not the emotional response he had expected from the question. After all, she was with her family and they seemed decent.

"Yes, Vitaly," she replied softly after a long pause.

"Really?" he asked, now suspecting otherwise.

She repositioned herself slightly, turning her body flat against his.

"Yes, but no is the honest answer," she replied with an uncertain smile.

"Yes, but no?" asked Vitaly with a confused chuckle as he gently twisted her fingers inside his and stroked her palm with his thumb absentmindedly.

"I love my family," she stated firmly and he waited expectantly for her to expand upon her answer. Upon realising she was finished, he spoke again.

"That much is obvious, Marta, but that wasn't my question," he explained as he looked into her eyes. She then dropped her head, placing her forehead onto his chest. Before he realised it, she had begun crying.

"Hey, what's wrong?" he asked with alarm as he removed his hand from hers, instead placing it gently on the back of her head and holding her against him warmly.

"I can't, Vitaly," she mumbled through her tears. "I can't leave here, regardless of how much I would like to," she added before looking up into his eyes. He looked back, smiled at her and then using his thumbs, wiped away the tears in her eyes.

"Why can't you leave here?" he asked tentatively as he

thought to himself how pretty she looked. "Will your father not let you?"

"Again, yes and no," she replied to Vitaly's look of confusion and growing annoyance.

"What does that mean?"

"It means that it's got nothing but also everything to do with my father," she replied with pursed lips.

Vitaly, with growing frustration, felt even more confused at her answer. What the hell is it about your father, he thought, imagining the kind but somewhat mysterious man he'd spent the day with. He searched and failed to find the answer in her saucer-like eyes so he had to ask.

"What about your father?" he asked, keeping his voice as level as possible and trying to mask his annoyance.

Perhaps seeing no way to placate him, she inhaled deeply and sighed. Then she answered him. "Do you realise who my father is?"

"What?"

"If you realised who he is, you'd understand my predicament. All of our predicaments, for that matter. It's not as simple as leaving and if you understood that, you'd leave here in the morning and forget the five mysterious people you met in the woods today."

Vitaly watched as her eyes began refilling with tears. She looked away, resting her head safely back down on his chest. Dare he ask? Perhaps he already knew?

"And who is your father?"

"I doubt you will believe me, Vitaly," came her muffled reply, very matter of fact.

"Why wouldn't I believe you, Marta?" he asked, reassuring her with a soft pat on her head. He followed by brushing away the hair that was covering her ear, exposing it. She turned and looked up, meeting his gaze with intensity.

"Okay," she replied. "My father is Nicholas Romanov II, Czar of Russia," she added, deadly serious.

Surprised, Vitaly's mouth dropped open. His mind clicked over as he waited patiently for her to either correct herself or crack and start laughing at him for indulging in her joke. Neither came.

Gathering himself, he asked, "Nicholas Romanov? The Czar?"

"That's correct," she replied, maintaining a straight face.

"But, but how could that be?" he stammered in response before he took a moment to consider things. "That would make you a Czarina!" He sat up and forced her to do the same. Marta secured the blanket around her as Vitaly then stood up and hastily tried to put on his pants. She had either failed to notice the scars on his leg or simply didn't care.

"There's no way I could ever sleep with a Czarina," he stammered, falling against the railing as his foot got stuck in his trouser leg. Regaining his balance, he refocused on her.

"You don't believe me?" she asked coyly as he stared at her.

"The Czar and his family were murdered, Marta!" replied Vitaly angrily. "They haven't been seen or heard from in over five years. Surely, if they were alive, even merely abroad, some word of their survival would have made its way around Russia. After all, despite the revolution, there are those here that remain loyal to them."

"A strategically fabricated lie agreed upon by my father the Czar," replied Marta coolly.

"What?" asked Vitaly in utter disbelief.

"We were marked to die," she replied with iciness.

"What?" Vitaly asked again, this time with repulsion.

Marta, now growing frustrated at Vitaly's lack of understanding and imagination and further annoyed at his failure to believe her, decided it was time for a full explanation.

"We were marked to die by the Bolsheviks," she said, her voice breaking this time as emotion washed over her. "After the abdication, we were prisoners of the provisional government under the watchful and protective eye of Alexander Kerensky…"

"Kerensky?"

"Yes, Kerensky. He was a surprisingly kind man," she added appreciatively and smiled.

"Kerensky?" asked Vitaly again disbelievingly. "What? I… I don't need to hear this, Marta," he stammered.

"Please, Vitaly, please don't interrupt me," she begged, suppressing tears. "It's hard enough to explain without interruptions." And she looked into his eyes imploringly. He became transfixed by her expression and was moved to silence by her big doe eyes. Nodding his understanding, she continued.

"There was a plan for us to be exiled abroad," she began. "England was the safest and therefore preferred choice. After all, King George is Papa's favourite cousin and they were as close as brothers. Everyone thought they looked alike, some even said they could be mistaken for twins. I wouldn't go that far, but I definitely noticed the similarities on our holiday to Cowes on the Isle of Wight fifteen years ago and subsequent to that, from photographs."

"That plan fell through though after Kerensky and the provisional government was overthrown by the Bolsheviks. Thankfully by that time, for our own safety, Kerensky had moved us to Tobolsk. While not disclosed to us, we noticed the difference in government via the attitudes of those assigned to guard us and their increasingly restrictive practices towards us."

"We spent several months in Tobolsk before we were moved to a house in Ekaterinburg. My father, mother and I were relocated first with my sisters and brother joining us later. My brother couldn't be moved initially due to ill health and my sisters were assigned to care for him until he had recovered."

"We spent nearly three months in that horrible house in Ekaterinburg before..." it was here Marta faltered, her voice breaking and being replaced by the sound of her soft sobs. Vitaly, moved by her emotion, fell to his knees and moved to embrace her. However, she reached out and placed an open palm on his bare chest, preventing him from doing so.

"Please don't, Vitaly. Please... please just let me finish first," she stammered through her tears.

"In that horrible house, our last night, we were summoned just after retiring for the evening. We were told to pack and escorted down into the basement on the pretence that we were being moved. We crowded in, all seven members of my family plus the four members of our household that accompanied us into exile. Dr Botkin, my mother's maid Anna, our cook Ivan and my father's valet Alexei."

"We waited there for ages before Yurovsky, our captor, returned with several of the guards and suddenly announced that we were to be exe... executed," she stammered before breaking down into more pronounced sobs and sniffling loudly.

Vitaly looked on with pity. He ached to hold her so badly it hurt. He wanted to tell her it was okay and reassure her that she was safe.

She continued, "I thought, we all thought we were going to die then and there. No chance of a goodbye, a last hug. It was a terrible shock. But then we were saved. Unbeknownst to us or Yurovsky and the other guards for that matter, the garrison had been infiltrated by some who were sympathetic to my father and our family."

She paused for several seconds, taking as many deep breaths as necessary to recover what composure she could before continuing. Vitaly looked at her and gently shook his head from side to side with disbelief, his eyes filled of sadness. He thought better of speaking. In truth, he didn't know what he could say. Then, steeling herself, she cleared her throat and continued.

"Latvians," she said loudly, her eyes boring into Vitaly's. "The two boys from the village were amongst them. There was a guard, he was Russian, a boy not much older than I," she said, smiling through her tears at the memory. "His name was Ivan and he was sweet and kind. For my nineteenth birthday he baked me a cake and brought it into the house."

"A few days later, he snuck me away into a room and we explored our feelings," she added, looking at her hands to hide her embarrassment. Vitaly understood. Looking back up, she continued as tears began to refill her eyes. "We were discovered and Ivan was sent away. I was afraid they would shoot him but I was later told he was imprisoned but not before he could feed information to our saviours on the outside."

"When Yurovsky and his men entered the basement, they lined up in front of us, the Latvians behind the Bolsheviks. Yurovsky announced our execution and then they all raised their pistols and aimed. Instead of shooting us though, the Latvian guards fired into the back of the Bolsheviks' skulls, killing them instead and saving us," she finished, sniffling and mumbling through the last sentence. Vitaly kneeled on the soft straw in front of her, hands resting on his thighs and feeling heartbroken.

"We were all in shock. In the confusion, the men then spoke briefly to my father before we were whisked outside through a doorway to a waiting lorry. I remember stepping over several bodies on the ground before being ordered to climb aboard into the back and driven away. We headed north, away from Ekaterinburg and into the woods. We drove for what felt like hours before we finally stopped at a crossroads where we were met by more men in another lorry."

"There we were ordered out and separated from the servants. They climbed aboard one lorry and the seven of us the other. I remember a guard speaking to us in French, reassuring us of our own and our servants' safety. Then we drove off on another long journey. I must have fallen asleep along the way, my siblings too, for the next thing I remember is waking up bathed in warm early morning sunshine. The lorry had stopped and the guards were spread out around us. They awoke everyone and ordered us down so the soldier in charge could talk to us."

"He was a Czech but he didn't speak Russian, English or French so the French guard we had encountered earlier translated. He explained that they were soldiers with the Czechoslovak Legion of the White army and had been commissioned to rescue the Imperial Family on behalf of King George the V and the British Government."

"We were to be transported north to Archangel where we would board a British navy warship and set sail out into the White Sea and down the coast of Norway. Then we would cross the North Sea to Aberdeen in Scotland before boarding a train to travel inland to Balmoral Castle where the King would be waiting to greet us."

"He told us that, despite now being in White-controlled territory, we were still in great danger. Our escape would be discovered despite their best efforts to conceal the truth and dispose of the evidence. Upon discovery, the Bolsheviks would likely strike back, beginning with the execution of other Romanov family members currently imprisoned. My parents enquired as to their safety but were rebuffed by the soldier and told that we were their priority, not our cousins, aunts and uncles."

"Despite my parents' protests, we climbed aboard the lorry again and began yet another arduous journey. The one that brought us here. That was five years ago. A temporary home that has become permanent due to the Civil War and subsequent Bolshevik victory. We're essentially trapped, joined here by the Latvian brothers who aided our escape and now help protect us from detection."

With the completion of the sentence, she broke down fully into tears as Vitaly embraced her tightly to which she offered no resistance. She briefly pulled away to open the blanket around her to allow Vitaly in, wrapping both her arms and the blanket securely back around him and concealing her tear-streaked face against his chest.

Her story had left Vitaly feeling ill. He stroked her hair as she continued to cry and as he did, he thought to himself, how could anyone conjure up a story like that? Least of all, this beautiful young woman. Russia had seen many horrors in the last decade; there was no reason this one couldn't be true. However, the Czar was rumoured to be dead. Rumoured, thought Vitaly. That was the key phrase.

Wait, no, that's incorrect, Vitaly thought to himself as a light went on in his memory. The Bolshevik government had announced his execution, he now recalled. He'd read that in the newspaper.

Could this man Feliks really be Nicholas II? Which would make Marta a Grand Duchess, he thought as he continued to hold her. The desire to believe her story was overpowering but the nagging voice, the voice of reason within his mind, remained doubtful. Sure, Feliks looked like the Czar, a point

Vitaly had made himself, though jokingly only a few hours earlier at dinner.

Marta pulled away to look up into his face. Her eyes, he noticed, were, if possible, even more saucer-like than before and despite them being swollen and red she remained very pretty. She stared into his eyes with intensity then leaned in and kissed him passionately on the lips. Kissing her back, he softly cradled her head in his hands before letting go as she pulled away.

She looked up again into his eyes, her own burning with the desire for him to understand, to believe and to accept. Then she asked tentatively the question he was afraid of. "Do you believe me?"

Authentication

The correct answer and immediate reply to her question should have been yes, but Vitaly lingered, his niggling doubt locked in an arm wrestle with the truth. In response, Marta's face dropped and her eyes began to fill again with tears.

"You don't believe me?" she asked softly, not meeting his eye.

"Marta, I..." he replied, unable to find the right words.

"I can prove it," she said forcefully and she released Vitaly from her arms and secured the rug tightly back around her. She reached out and grabbed the small pouch she'd earlier dropped onto the hay-strewn floor.

Turning back, she held it up to Vitaly before placing it down in front of her then reaching for her discarded sarafan. She then showed the sarafan to Vitaly before reaching into its pouch and producing a battered old budenovka cap. Holding the cap up, she dropped the sarafan and looked into his eyes and eagerly awaited his reaction.

Vitaly's face lit up. "Hey, that's my hat!" he exclaimed brightly, reaching out and taking it in his hand. "Where did you find it?" he asked before placing it on his head to ensure it fit and was therefore in fact his.

"Today in the woods on your head," she replied sharply.

"What?" he replied in kind, his expression becoming quizzical.

"I took it from your head earlier today in the woods and knocked your drinking cup over in the process I think," she replied, softening in her response due to embarrassment and offering him a sheepish smile.

Vitaly just stared at her, an amused smirk breaking across his face while she attempted to avoid his gaze.

"You were in the woods today?" he asked her gently.

Marta met his eyes and nodded gently, then upon seeing Vitaly's facial expression she too broke out into an amused smirk.

"I feel foolish, Vitaly," she smiled warmly, the tension between them dissipating. "It was fortuitous that I found you at all. The mushrooms that grow on the mossy banks along that stream are delicious so my sisters and I often walk out and collect them. Today it just happened to be me."

Vitaly laughed then smiled warmly at her. "Why did you take it? What would you want with my beaten old hat?"

Shrugging her shoulders, she replied, "I don't know. I panicked. You stirred at the wrong time and startled me I suppose. I was curious as to who you were. You looked beaten up but I presumed you must be kind after seeing you spare that beautiful doe."

"You saw that?" he asked, surprised and slightly embarrassed. "My father would kill me if he knew I'd let dinner escape," he added before amused chuckles from them both.

"Really?" she asked.

"Oh yes, we're peasants and the Bolsheviks take any excess

we can produce on the farm to the cities," he said, unable to disguise his bitterness. "Nevertheless, I couldn't bring myself to hurt such a beautiful creature," he finished before affectionately stroking Marta's soft cheek.

She reacted to his touch by gently pushing her face back against his open palm before looking up and meeting his eyes. She hesitated, reluctant to ask the question that rested upon her lips. "So, do you believe me, Vitaly?" she inquired softly. Once again, his reply wasn't forthcoming.

"You don't, do you?" she asked before shaking her head, the hurt and disappointment evident in her voice.

Resigned, Vitaly shook his head in confirmation.

She avoided his gaze and looked away. "Well, thankfully, like I said, I can prove it," she stated confidently. She picked up the small pouch resting in front of her. It was dark purple, made of what appeared to be silk and closed by two gold-threaded drawstrings that were tied into a bow. She pulled one and they both came undone, then using her index fingers she slowly pulled the pouch open.

She reached in, her hand closing securely around the possession inside before she began to slowly withdraw it. Once free of the pouch, which she dropped back to the ground again, she held it up in front of her for Vitaly to see. Whatever it was, was wrapped inside a silk handkerchief.

"There are few possessions that are more iconic, unique and valuable to the Imperial Family than what I hold in my hand here, Vitaly," Marta explained knowledgeably. "This such item was a gift presented to my mother by my father in 1895, just a few months after their marriage. I'm sure you've heard of them, perhaps you've even seen one before, likely in a photograph."

"What is it?" Vitaly asked.

Smiling at him sweetly, she began slowly unwrapping the

handkerchief to reveal a Fabergé egg. Vitaly's mouth dropped open. He'd heard of them, sure, however, he'd never actually believed they existed. Such opulence, such extravagance, such insurmountable wealth! He observed it closely, admiring how, even in this limited light, the innumerable number of jewels still sparkled brightly.

The immediate and most notable feature of this particular egg was its diamond-set Cupid's arrows symbolizing Love. It was crafted from multi-coloured gold and decorated with bands of rose-cut diamonds and covered with translucent red guilloché enamel. At its apex the egg had a miniature portrait of the young Emperor under a table-cut diamond, and at its base the date 1894.

Vitaly couldn't believe what he was seeing, then with a soft click, she opened it, revealing even more opulence. Contained within was a miniature diamond-set crown, a replica of the Imperial crown and a ruby drop.

"Marta, this, this is amazing," he scoffed, looking up into her eyes which now reflected the many jewels before them.

"I know, Vitaly, I know," she replied soothingly. "Perhaps now you believe me?" she asked again, more confident this time but still unsure of his reply. If this didn't prove her identity, nothing would.

"Yes," he said in response, smiling at her briefly before she dropped the rug and flung her arms around him in a tight embrace, pushing her bare breasts against his bare chest. He grunted in pain, alarming her.

"Oh, I'm sorry, Vitaly. Did I hurt you?"

"No, you didn't, but I must stop kneeling." He replied. "In all this excitement I've forgotten to straighten my leg," he said with a grimace.

She shifted herself to allow him to move into a sitting position before she repositioned herself safely in his lap. He gathered up the rug and wrapped her inside it before wrapping his arms around her securely.

She leaned back into him and rested her head on his shoulder as an overwhelming feeling of contentment and happiness washed over her. She held the egg and its contents in her outstretched hand, admiring its beauty through the moonlight.

"We could run away, Vitaly," she said. "This egg alone would buy us passage to any destination in the world and still leave us with more money than we'd need in a lifetime. Then of course there's the others, buried out there next to my mother and brother," she added, before turning to look at Vitaly and kissing him on the cheek.

"How many are there?" he asked with surprise.

"Fifty, I think, although we were forced to leave most of ours behind. Grandmama has several that she was given by my grandfather, Alexander III. Besides that, I don't know where they are now. I suppose the Bolsheviks have them. Here, Vitaly, why don't you hold it?"

"I um, okay," came his stammered reply, his face lighting up before taking it from her hand and holding it in his. It was surprisingly heavy, he guessed from the many diamonds and other jewels. He felt nervous. Never before and likely never again would he hold something of such monetary value in the palm of his hand.

He folded the top of the egg down and closed it to a light click as it locked shut. Handing it back to Marta, he watched as she placed it back into the drawstring pouch and tied the strings back into a bow.

"That is truly amazing," he explained, nuzzling her neck playfully. "Thank you for showing me."

"You're welcome," she replied before turning her head and kissing him passionately on the lips. After pulling away, she added, "Thank you for believing me," and smiled brightly at him.

"So, your real name is Maria, I'm guessing," stated Vitaly as they turned to look at each other. She giggled before nodding in confirmation. "I knew one of the Grand Duchesses was called Maria."

"That is correct," she replied sweetly. "I am Grand Duchess Maria Nikolaevna Romanova of Russia. My father Feliks is really Czar Nicholas II. My deceased mother is Alexandra Feodorovna and formerly Alix of Hesse. My sister Helga is Grand Duchess Olga, Tiana is Grand Duchess Tatiana and Anka is Grand Duchess Anastasia. My deceased little brother, Czarevich Alexei Nikolaevich, was the heir to the Imperial Russian Empire."

She wasn't saddened by the recollection; in fact, she was clearly pleased at being able to name her family members out loud. It must have been some time since she had done so, thought Vitaly. How sad. Being denied your identity. That burden would not have been easy. No wonder she wanted to leave. She wanted to be free again, he thought.

"Maria Nikolaevna Romanov," Vitaly repeated sweetly, whispering it into her ear. "It is a pleasure to finally meet you, your Imperial highness," he chuckled and she reached up and pulled him towards her for another kiss.

"I remember now," he exclaimed suddenly, upon surfacing for air.

Taken aback, Maria watched as his face lit up. "Remember? Remember what?"

"I remember where I've seen you before," he replied, smiling from the pleasant recollection.

Still confused, Maria asked, "From your dream?"

"Well, yes," he replied. "But I had my dream before I met you this afternoon."

Maria, continuing to look confused, waited expectantly for an explanation. Meanwhile, Vitaly rubbed the top of his head in thought.

"And are you going to explain?" asked Maria impatiently.

"It was at the Winter Palace in Petrograd," he explained. "I had been transferred to the hospital there to have my injuries treated and convalesce."

"The scars on your legs?"

"Yes," he replied, smiling. "You, your sisters and your mother paid a visit. Actually, one of your sisters might've nursed me. I can't recall."

"As Papa explained earlier, both Olga and Tatiana were nurses with the Red Cross. Mama too," interrupted Maria.

"Well then, I possibly met all three," Vitaly remarked pleasantly. "But I specifically remember speaking to you," he smiled. "You spoke to me for several minutes and actually sat on the edge of my bed, much to the shock and disapproval of your mother," he recalled, chuckling at the memory.

"Yes, I remember now," added Maria sweetly, her face contorted in memory. "Mama had been distracted by another soldier, nurse, or doctor. I can't remember which exactly but she was aghast when she turned around to find me sitting on the side of your bed," she explained as Vitaly chuckled.

"It wasn't funny!" she said, slapping Vitaly softly on his thigh and causing them both to laugh.

"You did however make the mistake of bumping, albeit accidentally, my injured leg and throwing me into a fit of pain and an impressive exhibition of expletives," Vitaly said, teasingly.

"Yes, I remember that too. I also remember apologising profusely and you in turn apologising profusely. I felt terrible. Then you flirted with me and told me how beautiful you thought I was," she said, turning to meet Vitaly's eyes and putting her lovely saucers on full display before kissing him again.

Vitaly, arms still wrapped around Maria, lay down on his back and pulled Maria down with him so she was once again lying on top of him. She turned over and rested her head comfortably on his chest and covered them both with the blanket as they continued to caress and kiss each other.

"I've had a wonderful evening, Maria," stated Vitaly softly, whispering into her ear. She looked up at him and smiled. "But it's late and unfortunately, I have a long walk ahead of me tomorrow. While I can assure you, I don't want this to end, I must sleep," he added reluctantly. "I would like and very much hope that you will spend the night here with me."

She looked at him and smiled, then in almost a whisper she said, "I'm not going anywhere!"

"And what about in the morning?" asked Vitaly tentatively.

"What do you mean?"

"Will we exit the barn together in the morning?"

"Yes," she replied, unconcerned. "Hand in hand."

Vitaly smiled. "And what will your father think?"

"Regarding what?"

"Of you spending the night with me here in the barn."

"Honestly, Vitaly, I don't care," she replied with conviction.

"Your reputation will be ruined, Maria," he replied with amusement.

"And I don't care," she replied. "The Romanov reputation is ruined and I want to run away. I want freedom, fun, adventure, family, children and security," she added with passion.

"And you want to run away with me?" asked Vitaly, his heart racing in anticipation of an answer.

"Yes, Vitaly, I do!" she replied before kissing him on the lips.

"What about poverty?" he added with uncertainty after pulling away.

"If it equates to freedom, I don't care. Besides, I have the egg and it's worth a lifetime of fun and adventure followed by a home and a family," she stated confidently.

With that, Vitaly kissed her on the cheek approvingly and squeezed her body softly. "Good night, Maria," he said softly.

"Good night Vitaly," she replied in kind, and they rearranged themselves into spoons before they slowly drifted off to sleep.

Disappointment

For the third time in a row, Vitaly's dreams were absent of the horrors of war. His cousin was brought back to life again and they laughed and joked while they sat around the izba's warm stove. Pyotr and Lena were there, Anatoly, Irina and Sofia too, but most importantly, Maria.

They had children now, three little ones. The boy, the oldest, rested against his father's legs and nursed a Russian wolfhound pup while his twin sisters toddled around their mother and grandmother's legs, competing for which lap to sit on in a comical variation of musical chairs.

Maria picked up one of their daughters and smiled across the room at her husband, Grandmama Lena doing the same. Both took a little girl's hand and waved it at their father. Vitaly almost burst with happiness, matching emotions with his young wife. He couldn't help but notice his daughter's eyes. They were both a beautiful blue and like saucers.

Before his eyes materialised four more children which he knew instinctively belonged to Evgeny and Sofia, who were now also joined by their respective wife and husband. He didn't know Evgeny's wife but she was beautiful and he watched her with curiosity as she pulled up a chair and joined Maria and Lena seated at the kitchen table before picking up and holding one of her own little daughters.

Sofia's husband was familiar to him so he presumed he must be Edgar Tarlov, who she had mentioned to him only yesterday. She must have said yes to his proposal and started her own little family. Her two sons now joined Vitaly's and began playing with their cousin and his wolfhound pup. They were all happy and content.

Then the dream changed. He was no longer surrounded by his family and seated in and around their family's izba; instead, he was standing hand in hand with Maria in a large ornate palace ballroom. This is what a palace looks like? he thought in amazement as a waltz began playing and those standing closest to him bowed and curtsied to the couple as they slowly made their way through the crowd towards the centre of the polished marble dancefloor.

He looked down and admired his fashionable tuxedo and white gloved hands, then up at his wife, who shone in a beautiful flowing white evening gown. She smiled back at him, her eyes dancing and filled with happiness. He smiled back and despite not knowing how, began swinging Maria around in large circles which were perfectly in sync with the music.

They danced for ages, until Feliks, no, it was Nicholas now, the Czar, he approached and asked his daughter's hand for a dance. Vitaly accepted happily and Nicholas beamed at them both. As he watched the two Romanovs dance together a pain began in the back of his head that ran all the way down his back. It was dull at first but quickly increased in intensity.

He looked up at the ornate ceiling, which slowly became

unfocused, then looked around the large room and met the same effect. He knew what was happening, his dream was collapsing and he felt disappointed. It had been another good one.

What he didn't understand though, was why it was painful. Perhaps he had rolled into an uncomfortable position and Maria had somehow rolled onto him or perhaps accidentally hit him in her sleep. The stack of hay in the barn was soft and comfortable, Maria too, so then what was the cause?

The scene began to shake and suddenly the crowd parted and Maria came running towards him, her long gown billowing out behind her. Her face was tear-streaked before she reached him and when she did, she wrapped her arms around him tightly before kissing him passionately. Looking into each other's eyes longingly, she spoke.

"This is it, Vitaly," she said loudly, followed by a sniffle as the room shook violently. The guests standing around them watched on curiously before they suddenly disappeared.

"It's just a dream," he replied consolingly while he smiled down at her.

"No, Vitaly, this is it," she repeated forcefully, and there was sadness in her eyes.

"It's just a dream, Maria," he assured her again. "We're asleep in each other's arms in a haystack in the barn. Well, you wouldn't know that of course. One person can't enter another person's dream," he finished, smiling reassuringly.

"No, Vitaly, no. THIS. IS. IT. This is the end!" she exclaimed before she released him from her arms and stepped back, much to his dismay. The room shook again, this time as if an earthquake had struck it and she looked back at him with tear-filled eyes.

"Goodbye, Vitaly," she said, choking out the words as he looked back at her, confused. "I love you," she added, managing to smile through her tears and blowing him a final kiss before, with one last and violent shake, the dream turned to black and Vitaly awoke.

Absent of the soft warm touch of Marias body and the cushioned surface of the hay, the back of his head ached, his back too and for some reason he was sitting up and resting against something odd-shaped and uncomfortable. Alarm bells began to ring and his eyes jolted open.

He was blinded by the light and lifted his arm to shield his eyes from it. He was no longer in the barn but outdoors somewhere. Finally, his eyes adjusted and he was able to look around comfortably only to discover that he was back in the woods and sitting once again, beneath the large fir tree.

Upon the realisation, he felt as if someone had punched him in the stomach. He became short of breath and inhaled with difficulty. He forced himself up and looked around in alarm. His bag lay by his side but nothing else was littered around so he picked it up and slung it over his shoulder. He knew what he had to do.

However, he felt sick again and pressed a hand against the fir tree in support as his breathing slowly returned to normal. "No. No, no, no, no, no, no," he said to himself softly, comprehending what had happened, or not happened in the last twelve hours. "No. No, no, no, no, NO, NOOOO!" he screamed at the top of his lungs as his anguished voice reverberated around the dense woods.

He forced himself upright and turned in the direction of the clearing where he had discovered Feliks – or Nicholas, or whatever his name was – and began in that direction. Following the stream, he forced himself along, recognising the path to take from earlier – today? Yesterday? In his dream? He was unsure. His leg ached and was particularly stiff, but then, his entire body was.

Before long, he reached the sunlit clearing and raced out to inspect it but found nobody there. Reassuringly though, there were several freshly felled logs and numerous blocks scattered around carelessly. This, along with the realisation that his hat was once again back on his head and his elbow was bandaged, buoyed his hopes. "That definitely happened then," he said to himself quietly.

"MARIA!" he yelled. Then "FELIKS!" Followed by "NICHOLAS!" for good measure, startling all the birds in the surrounding trees and causing them to take flight. Best not leave any stone unturned. "MARIA!? MARTA!? WHERE ARE YOU!?" he screamed again. But there was no response. With a deep breath, he willed himself on down the path through the trees and into the woods towards their izba.

He danced over and around exposed tree roots, occasionally stumbling on one that was obscured by a particularly dark shadow. He turned left where the road split and followed fresh wheel tracks in the dry soil. He passed along the eroded bank of the stream and soon enough could make out the clearing in the woods through the trees. The stone chimney of the izba, set with clay, rose into the sky imposingly beyond.

He crossed into the clearing, exposing himself to the warm sunlight. He looked to his right and there rested three grave markers, the closest one reading Alexei. But the izba looked different. The woven fence was broken, the gravel driveway and vegetable garden overgrown. The front windows were smashed, the door missing, torn from its hinge and the stairway collapsed. Looking down the driveway, there was only the burnt-out shell of a barn remaining.

Something had gone terribly wrong. But what? "MARIA!"

Vitaly yelled out, followed again by "Feliks" and "Nicholas" but again no response came. Vitaly looked around feverishly then hobbled towards the front door, dropped his bag from his shoulder and lifted himself up and over the lip to find himself looking into the dilapidated izba. "MARIA!" he screamed yet again and again received no reply. He was getting desperate now.

He turned and jumped down, landing but falling to the ground beneath his weakened and injured leg. He cried out in pain but forced himself up again and hobbled around the corner and down the drive towards the barn as fast as his aching body would carry him. Arriving where the door once stood, he rested a hand on the frame and looked around tentatively, frightened at the prospect of what he might find. "MARIA!" he called again. Silence.

He tentatively stepped into what remained of the barn and carefully inspected the contents. He reached the location of the stall he and Maria had fallen asleep in together the night before – or at least he thought they had – and pulled what debris he could aside before inspecting it. Disappointment and relief washed over him. She wasn't here. "MARIA!" he called again, and again he received no response.

Where else was there to look? he thought. It looked as if nobody had lived here for months, perhaps years. But how could that be? He had literally slept in this very spot only last night. What had happened in the interim? Had the Vyatka horse knocked over a lantern? But that wouldn't explain how he came to be back under that fir tree.

Perhaps he had been drugged? Feliks? He meant Nicholas, perhaps. Had the discovery of Vitaly and his daughter caused him to go into a rage? But why would he move him, unconscious, back into the woods? No, that couldn't be it. He wouldn't lose control so badly that he would burn down their own barn and ransack their izba.

Maybe members of the local Soviet, Karasev's comrades, Vorshenko and Denisov? Perhaps they had been able to track him here in the night and attacked. But again, why would they move him into the woods and coincidentally to that exact spot? Surely, they would've arrested him. No, none of this made sense.

He turned and looked back down the driveway before carefully retracing his steps through and out of the barn. He was thirsty and remembered he'd dropped his bag by the front door and began walking back towards it. He felt like crying as he looked out across the now empty field to his left. Maria was gone, but where? How could she just disappear? He was overcome with doubt about the reality of her existence. Had it all just been a dream? Granted, a very realistic and vivid one?

He rounded the corner of the izba and spotted his bag. Reaching it, he retrieved his canteen and drank thirstily before slowly turning in a circle and inspecting the entire clearing. Alas, from the woods behind the barn all the way down to the riverbank there was nothing and nobody to be found.

With resignation, he drained his canteen and resecured the lid. Bending down, he picked up his bag and opened it before roughly stuffing it back inside. As he did, something caught his eye. A single strand of gold-coloured thread, something he knew he didn't possess, glinted faintly in the dim light from within. His curiosity piqued, he reached in and closed his hand around what felt like a silken pouch.

He slowly withdrew it before holding it up to the light and immediately recognising the pouch as the one belonging to Maria. It was dark purple and secured with the golden threat that was tied into a neat bow. He instinctively knew what was inside judging by its weight, rounded shape and both smooth and bumpy surfaces.

He looked at it in amazement but suddenly found himself doubtful as to its contents. Surely not! But there was only one way to find out, and that was to open it. However, that would also make this real, which further contradicted the present situation. Holding it in one hand, he carefully pulled one of the strings and it came undone. Using his thumb and forefinger, he teased it open and looked inside.

If it could, extravagance would've stared straight back at him to find a young man with his mouth hanging open in amazement. There in his palm rested the Rosebud Egg, forged by Fabergé as a symbol of the love between Czar Nicholas II and his wife, Alexandra of Hesse. Maria had held this in her small soft palm only hours ago and had somehow managed to sneak it into his bag. But how?

Then that makes this all real? Vitaly thought quietly. But again, how? He continued to ponder the answer as he withdrew the egg from the pouch to hold it in his bare hand. It was quite the spectacle in the sunlight. Every surface lit up, sparkled and reflected the sun beautifully. It was truly iridescent.

Vitaly was absorbed by its beauty, but saddened by its procurement. Did this mean Maria was gone? Her family too? Perhaps they had moved on? Was this her parting gift? Again, that didn't explain anything and he exhaled loudly with frustration.

He thought he heard his name being called and span around quickly. Off in the distance, down the road away from the clearing, a man was approaching. A tall man and of considerable girth. Hastily, Vitaly returned the egg to its pouch, drew the strings and tied them securely back into a bow before carefully returning it to his bag.

He looked up again to discover the man had made considerable ground and was closing in fast. However, he recognised him and was flooded with a feeling of relief. It was the Bear – Comrade Anya.

"Vitaly?" he called out, following it with a congenial wave. "I've been looking for you."

The Saviour

Puffing and panting, the Bear came to a stop in front of Vitaly. He stood there in silence and drew several deep breaths, inspecting Vitaly closely as he did. Vitaly, wearing a bemused smile, did the same back.

The Bear noticed Vitaly's bandaged elbow, bruised temple, scratched arms and general dishevelled appearance which caused him to furrow his eyebrows disapprovingly. What had happened to this boy in the last forty-eight hours?

"Are you okay?" he asked with concern, causing Vitaly to look himself up and down.

"I think so," replied Vitaly casually, brushing away some dried dirt he'd noticed from the front of his shirt.

"What the hell happened to you?"

Detecting some annoyance in the question, Vitaly replied light-heartedly, "Rough couple of days." before smiling weakly.

"Where have you been?" asked the Bear impatiently.

"In the woods," replied Vitaly shortly, pointing over his shoulder with his free hand. He knew that! It'd been him who'd told him to go there in the first place.

"No, no, no... Well, yes, but that's not what I meant," stammered the Bear while Vitaly looked back at him incredulously. "I mean," continued the Bear, "what do I mean?" and he stopped for another second to think. Meanwhile, Vitaly slung his bag back over his shoulder and continued to look at comrade Anya, this time with confusion.

"What I mean is, tell me what happened to you?" explained the Bear. "Why did you run away from me at your uncle's?"

"That was you!?" asked Vitaly indignantly, his temper suddenly rising.

"Yes. Myself and comrade Kasaev," replied the Bear coolly despite Vitaly's expression of disbelief.

"I ran because you fucking shot at me!" he responded angrily, raising his voice accordingly and clenching his fists. The Bear, noticing, took a precautionary step backwards.

"I didn't shoot at you, nor did Kasaev," replied the Bear calmly. "It was your uncle who fired the gun," he continued. "He tried to shoot Kasaev."

"Kasaev!? What!? I heard the shot go over my head," replied Vitaly in disbelief.

"Yes, Kasaev was chasing you," explained the Bear with composure. "We'd hoped to catch you before you disappeared into the woods. Misunderstanding the situation, Anatoly shot at him while he was in pursuit of you," he finished before offering Vitaly an apologetic and somewhat sheepish smile.

"Misunderstood the situation?" replied Vitaly sarcastically, rolling his eyes. "Who the fuck turns up at someone's izba in a car in Kyrubol in the middle of the night!? It's very suspicious! So naturally we thought it was the fucking Bolsheviks come to drag me away for what I did to Karasev!" he finished, spitting on the ground in front of him.

The Bear watched him intently, still careful to maintain a

safe distance. His face had become expressive and displayed a look of empathy for the ordeal he had obviously, though inadvertently, put Vitaly through over the last two days. Meanwhile, everything that had happened in that time was bubbling to the surface now inside Vitaly and although he knew this man was not really to blame, he was nonetheless enraged.

"I'm sorry, Vitaly," the Bear said remorsefully as his face slackened. "You've obviously had a tough couple of days out here," he added solemnly, "and that's my fault." He looked at the ground in a gesture of atonement.

"Hmm!" came Vitaly's exasperated reply, followed by a deep sigh. He was even more annoyed now. Annoyed at allowing himself to be so easily disarmed by the Bear, this gentle giant who had probably saved his life. Suddenly the feeling of guilt crept in as a voice in the back of his head asked him how he could be so ungrateful.

"No, no, it's not your fault, Anya," said Vitaly softly, followed by another deep sigh. He unclenched his fists and began to feel his temper ebbing away. "I'm sorry and grateful for your help the other day."

The Bear, with a warm smile, began, "regarding that, the other day. Your parents are okay," he said with satisfaction and instantly, Vitaly's attention was redirected.

"They are?"

"Yes, they're fine," replied the Bear. "Your uncle, aunt and cousin too."

"Thank you for that," replied Vitaly, relieved, tipping the front of his cap appreciatively.

"You're welcome, comrade," replied the Bear jovially. "But I have other news. Good news! News that will please you greatly!"

"What news?"

"You're keeping your farm, and the same goes for your uncle and aunt," explained the Bear. "The whole village too!"

Vitaly's eyes lit up. "What? How?" he asked excitedly.

"As it turns out, Karasev and those other members of the local Soviet, Vorshenko and Denisov for example, have been engaging in corruption," explained the Bear with satisfaction as Vitaly listened in attentive silence. "The farm requisitions are only one of many examples of this. Konstantin Karlov's mill is another, but there are many, many more."

"And what of Karasev?" asked Vitaly excitedly.

"Currently?" said the Bear coyly.

"Yes."

"Currently he is under guard in the hospital at Ekaterinburg where he shall remain until he is well enough to travel by train to Moscow. Once there, he shall receive a trial," explained the Bear with a grin. "You really did a number on him," he added, imitating a boxing stance and swinging several playful punches.

"I don't regret that so much now," replied Vitaly with a satisfied smile.

"Nor should you," replied the Bear. "I can personally assure you that you will receive no punishment or reprimand for your actions either."

"Really?" asked Vitaly, relieved as the good news kept coming thick and fast. "How can you be so sure?"

"Because, and I'm going to let you in on a little secret here, my friend. I'm a member of the Cheka and have been investigating what was suspected corruption inside the local Soviet for months now."

"You're Cheka? The secret police?" asked Vitaly cautiously.

"That's correct, comrade," replied the Bear reassuringly. "Although there is no need to be afraid," he continued quickly, noticing Vitaly's expression.

"I've heard many things about the Cheka," exclaimed Vitaly apprehensively, causing the Bear to smile.

"I suspect most Russians have," replied the Bear ruefully. "Unfortunately, there are those amongst the Cheka that are, let me say, less than desirable. There are those too that believe in serving their Russian brothers and sisters faithfully. The lines get blurred, but thankfully, Vladimir Lenin is serious about squashing out dissent and making his new Russia work," he finished proudly.

"What do you think of Lenin? Do you know him?" asked Vitaly, boldly.

The Bear nodded. "Not well, but I have met him and spoken with him," he explained. "He assigned me this task as I'm familiar with the area having grown up here."

"I thought you looked familiar!" said Vitaly.

"Yes, we attended school together," replied the Bear quickly. "And your mother taught me," he added in acknowledgment. "Although there are a few years between us, I think. Me being the older."

"Yes, I remember now," replied Vitaly. "You were finishing when I was beginning."

"That sounds correct," replied the Bear.

"What's your first name?"

"Christophe."

"My father and I referred to you as the Bear the other day."

"Really?" replied the Bear with a chuckle. "I like that actually," he added approvingly. "Due to my size, I suppose?"

"Yes, Christophe," replied Vitaly, followed by a chuckle of his own.

"Christophe Anya," exclaimed Vitaly thoughtfully. "You left Virubol only to return years later as a member of the Cheka," he finished, meeting his comrade's eyes and searching his face thoughtfully. "How did you find me? Or, rather, how did you know I'd be here?"

"I heard you yelling," replied the Bear as he looked at the ransacked izba with concern. "Who is Maria?" he asked, again meeting Vitaly's eye.

Vitaly was surprised at the question and stumbled in reply. "I, um, I don't truthfully know," he stammered back uncertainly, piquing the Bear's interest.

"You don't know?" he asked suspiciously. "Yet you were screaming her name? That is interesting," he added, continuing to eye Vitaly, which was making him nervous. What was he going to say? thought Vitaly, and how would he explain who Maria was if the Bear pushed him for details? Thankfully, the Bear moved on to another question.

"Did you sleep here last night?" he asked after again inspecting the izba.

"Ah, I, I don't know," admitted Vitaly, shaking his head in defeat at not knowing what to say. He met the Bear's eyes again and could tell he didn't believe him. Was this how Maria had felt when she was trying to explain things to him.

"I'm confused here, Vitaly," stated the Bear patiently. "You don't know if you slept here last night?" he asked incredulously whilst pointing to the izba.

"No, I don't," replied Vitaly quickly.

"Well, it's certainly not Buckingham Palace," replied the Bear with amusement before he turned all the way around and faced the missing front door. "Still, it offers some, if only minimal, protection from the elements," he added before turning back to Vitaly and looking him up and down before refocusing on the large bruise on his temple.

"That looks painful," he stated with concern, and Vitaly gently nodded in agreement. "When I return you to the farm, I will collect a doctor to take a look at you. And your elbow? How did you manage to bandage it?" the Bear asked, looking impressed.

"I, um, I didn't," replied Vitaly uncertainly as he looked down and flexed the limb carefully, the Bear watching on patiently for him to elaborate. Vitaly looked up and met his eye again but could only manage an awkward smile.

"You didn't bandage it, did you?" asked the Bear knowingly.

Looking sheepish, Vitaly replied, "No, I didn't."

"Then who did, Vitaly?" asked the Bear with suspicion. "Was it Maria?"

"No," replied Vitaly quickly as he looked around nervously.

"Then who, Vitaly?" asked the Bear, his frustration beginning to show.

"You won't believe me," replied Vitaly, becoming serious, "and you'll think I'm crazy," he added, studying the Bear's face. He looked frustrated but curious.

"Then test me, comrade," the Bear responded kindly.

"Okay," replied Vitaly with scepticism before shrugging his shoulders.

"Go on then," said the Bear, nodding his approval before Vitaly took a deep breath and let out another deep sigh.

"After I ran away from my uncles," he started, "I became lost in the woods and wandered for hours. Eventually I needed a rest so I sat down under a tree and fell asleep. I was awoken by the sound of a woodcutter chopping wood and being in the state that I was, I decided to follow the sound and seek him out. I figured, perhaps he could help me?" He shrugged his shoulders again while the Bear watched on, transfixed.

"But I was hesitant. I didn't know if he was friendly or possibly on the look-out for me. He was in a clearing a couple of kilometres back there in the woods. I approached and surprised him but we got talking and he offered to take me to his home where he lived with his four daughters, two of whom were nurses, and I needed medical attention. The cut on my elbow was bad but it was my head that he was most concerned about.

"He then drove us here to this clearing but the izba wasn't like this." Vitaly turned to look at it. "It was intact, neat and tidy, and true to his word, occupied by himself and his four daughters, who greeted us as we drove his troika into the barn back there." He pointed around the izba towards the burnt-out barn.

"After introductions, we headed inside for dinner and then afterwards his daughters stitched and bandaged my wound and inspected my head."

"Maria was one of them?" interrupted the Bear.

"She was there, but she wasn't a nurse, nor was the other one, Anka or Anastasia," replied Vitaly.

"Anka or Anastasia?" asked the Bear thoughtfully. "You don't remember their names?"

"No, I remember them, and I'll explain in a moment," replied Vitaly impatiently. "Where was I? Oh yes, after that, I accompanied Feliks."

"Feliks?"

"The man's name was Feliks. The father of the four women," replied Vitaly, again with impatience. "We went outside and walked down to the little graveyard there in the distance, next to the road at the edge of the trees." He pointed in its direction. "His wife and son are buried there," explained Vitaly before he abruptly stopped talking and became lost in thought.

"Yes?" asked the Bear with anticipation.

"Alexandra and Alexei," stated Vitaly, almost in a whisper.

"What, Vitaly? I can't hear you."

"Yes, Alexandra and Alexei are buried there," replied Vitaly, speaking normally again, although his voice belied the fact that his mind was somewhere else. "He told me how they died before we walked back to the izba and I headed to the barn where I was spending the night. Last night," he added quickly, correcting himself as he met the Bear's eye.

"And?" the Bear asked, engrossed.

"I went to sleep before being awoken by Maria."

"And?" asked the Bear again.

"We made love," explained Vitaly with a satisfied smile.

The Bear, disregarding this last fact, looked again at the izba before taking several steps along the gravel road, passing Vitaly and stopping to look up the overgrown driveway at the burnt-out barn. Inspecting it, he then looked back.

"You slept in there?" he asked incredulously. "Last night?"

"Yes," replied Vitaly with conviction as the Bear shook his head in disbelief.

"Tell me, Vitaly, about the names," he asked. "You sounded unsure."

"Perhaps it was just a dream," Vitaly said uncertainly. "Because, I woke up about an hour ago back under that tree," he explained. "But how can that be?" he asked the Bear optimistically. Maybe he could make sense of it.

"What were the people's names?" pressed the Bear. "It's important that you remember."

"That's the most unbelievable part yet," Vitaly said, forcing a laugh.

"Go on."

"I was introduced to Feliks as Feliks but Maria told me his real name was Nicholas," stated Vitaly, before allowing a minute for the significance of that to sink in. However, the Bears expression didn't change so Vitaly continued, "The daughters were introduced to me as Helga, Tiana, Marta and

Anka but their real names were Olga, Tatiana, Maria and Anastasia," he explained.

The Bear's eyes bulged. He'd understood, thought Vitaly confidently. But did he believe him? The Bear looked at him with curiosity, which came as a relief to Vitaly, although, truthfully, what had he been expecting?

"You understand the significance of those names?" asked the Bear, looking at him thoughtfully.

"Yes, I understand," replied Vitaly, worried what would happen next.

"Allow me to explain something to you, Vitaly," said the Bear very seriously. "My advice, which I have given to you before faithfully, is, when we leave this clearing, mention nothing of the people you met here, ever – to no one!"

"But why?" asked Vitaly, confused.

"Because there were people here, Vitaly," replied the Bear.

"Who? Who lived here?" asked Vitaly pressingly, but the Bear pressed a finger to his lips and shook his head vigorously. He approached Vitaly and leant in, before, in little more than a whisper, he replied to his question.

"About five years ago a family of seven came to live here," explained the Bear cautiously.

"Was it the Romanovs?" asked Vitaly, expecting the Bear to be surprised, but instead he simply smiled.

"Yes," he said softly.

"Five years ago, you said?" asked Vitaly.

"That's correct."

"Then how come I saw them last night? That doesn't make sense!"

"You must have been dreaming," replied the Bear.

"If I was dreaming, how do you explain this?" replied Vitaly, and he removed his bag and reached in to retrieve the

Fabergé egg. He removed it from its silk pouch and watched as the Bear's eyes bulged in disbelief.

Holding it in his palm between them, the Bear asked, "How did you get that?"

"The girl, Maria. She showed it to me last night in the barn there!" stated Vitaly, pointing at the empty burnt-out shell.

"No, that can't be," said the Bear softly, shaking his head.

"It can't, but it is," replied Vitaly.

"The Romanovs are long gone," explained the Bear. "Their jewels and other possessions either abroad in the hands of their many relatives or securely locked away in the Kremlin Armoury under the ever watchful and suspicious eyes of the Bolsheviks."

"Then how?" asked Vitaly.

"I don't know, comrade," replied the Bear sincerely. "But I would hide this somewhere safe. Bury it even."

"You won't take it?" asked Vitaly reluctantly as the Bear met his eye.

"It was given to you, wasn't it?"

"Less given, more left in my bag."

"Then keep it," replied the Bear dismissively. "The Bolsheviks likely think it lost," he added. "Of the many eggs that were crafted, there are several that are missing. This must be one of them. Trust me, they won't miss it."

"But what will I do with it?" asked Vitaly.

"Like I said, hide it, bury it, somewhere safe though. It would be dangerous to be found with it. Much more than your farm would be taken from you."

"I will throw it into the woods," replied Vitaly earnestly.

"And you would be throwing away a lifetime's fortune," replied the Bear.

"You literally just said to hide it and bury it," replied Vitaly sharply.

"It's not the same thing. Hide it until you can leave Russia then sell it once you're abroad."

"But I don't want to leave Russia," replied Vitaly, pleadingly.

"You will comrade, eventually," replied the Bear solemnly and his face filled with sadness. "Vladimir Lenin is unwell and the man most likely to succeed him is a monster."

"What? How do you know this?"

"It was Lenin who assigned me this task, remember?" replied the Bear with exasperation. "And I've seen him with my own two eyes."

"What's wrong with him?" asked Vitaly with eagerness.

"I shouldn't be telling you this but I'll put my misguided faith in you to remain silent," replied the Bear, smiling wryly.

"I can keep a secret!" replied Vitaly with indignation.

"I'm sure you can, Vitaly," replied the Bear. "However, some are more dangerous than others."

"I can keep a secret," reiterated Vitaly, "and if the information can help keep my family safe, I'd like to know."

"Very well then, comrade," replied the Bear. "Lenin has suffered a debilitating stroke and it is likely he will die."

"I must say, comrade Lenin has had some considerable misfortune," replied Vitaly with surprise. "Although, I suppose it wasn't misfortune that helped him survive the assassination attempt by that anarchist Kaplan. But what does his death mean for Russia?"

"It means that Joseph Stalin will be his most likely successor," replied the Bear with trepidation. "And Stalin is the most dangerous man in all of Russia."

"I've heard of him," stated Vitaly.

"I suspect you have, comrade," replied the Bear. "Even for a Bolshevik he is radical and violent. When he ascends to power, and he will, he will purge this country of all opposition.

Anyone who opposes him or stands in his way is already in danger without yet realising it. If you can't say you're loyal, then you best flee. The sooner the better," he finished with a curt nod.

"Am I to understand then that I should take this precious egg and flee Russia before Lenin dies?" asked Vitaly.

"Yes, my friend. That is exactly what I am advising you to do," the Bear replied. "Take your parents, your uncle, aunt and cousin with you and flee. Forget the farm, trust me."

"Then will you please take me there? Back to the farm?" asked Vitaly with the subtlest hint of panic in his voice.

"Of course," replied the Bear, taken aback. "Are you up to a short walk back down the road?"

"Yes, I'll be fine," replied Vitaly assuredly.

"Very well then comrade, if you'll follow me, I'll take you home." Smiled the Bear before reaching out and patting Vitaly gently on the shoulder. Then, pointing in the direction from whence he came, both men turned and began to walk slowly down the road before they eventually disappeared from view around a bend in the distance.

Reunited

The two men reached the Fiat, which Vitaly recognised instantly as the same one that had been parked outside his parents' farm the other day. Today however, the Bear was alone and would be playing the part of chauffeur.

Vitaly came to a rest against the vehicle's passenger side fender panel and waited for the Bear to open the front door before helping him inside. Once he was seated comfortably, the Bear gently shut the door again and rounded the vehicle to the driver's side.

Stopping, he leant down on the driver's door window sill and observed his passenger wincing in pain. "Are you sure you're okay, Vitaly?" he asked.

"Yes, yes," replied Vitaly through gritted teeth. "My knee just seized up. It does that sometimes."

"After what your body's been through these last couple of days it's no surprise," replied the Bear sympathetically.

"Just get me home, please Anya," replied Vitaly shortly, "and please drive carefully. I don't think I can handle being bounced around."

"I'll do my best," replied the Bear as he opened the door and seated himself behind the wheel. He slammed the door shut and gunned the engine. It roared to life, abruptly shattering the quiet ambiance.

To his credit, the Bear was a cautious driver. However, that alone didn't stop him from hitting several potholes and causing Vitaly multiple spasms of pain. The problem was the primitive nature of the roadway which was rough and ungraded and up until a few years ago had been frequented exclusively by horse and cart.

They reached an intersection and turned left onto another gravel roadway, this one being wider and of a much better grade. Vitaly was appreciative of the smoother surface and engaged the Bear in conversation again, hopeful of the distraction it would bring.

"You suggest leaving Russia like it's a decision made on a whim," he stated loudly in an effort to be heard over the roar of the Fiat's engine. The roof was down too, which allowed a pleasant breeze to ruffle his hair but was a further impediment to their conversation. "And go where exactly?"

"England, America, Australia, Canada," replied the Bear succinctly, chancing a quick sideways glance at Vitaly before refocusing his eyes on the road.

Vitaly sat quietly in thought for a moment, then replied, "England is too small, my parents would hate it there!"

"Then take your pick from the other three," replied the Bear dismissively.

"America is the land of opportunity and geographically enormous," stated Vitaly thoughtfully. "Perhaps we could purchase some farm land somewhere in the middle?"

"An excellent idea," replied the Bear enthusiastically.

"I know little if anything of Australia or Canada," replied

Vitaly. "Canada borders America to the north, is covered extensively in forest and extremely cold."

"Australia is hot, dry and dusty but largely unsettled," replied the Bear knowledgeably. "It was originally colonized by the British and consists today of their descendants, the remaining native aborigines, some Chinese and a few Arabs," he continued. "Canada is known for being cold, yes, but its winters are very similar to our own. It shares a border with Alaska which once belonged to Russia until Alexander II sold it to America sixty years ago to help pay for the Crimean War."

Impressed, Vitaly looked at the Bear and watched with interest as he geared the Fiat down to cross a shallow ford. The sound of the parting water was audible over the growl of the engine before the Bear accelerated up a small incline and raced away.

"Are you sure about Stalin?" asked Vitaly.

"I'm sure, comrade," replied the Bear solemnly, watching the road. "It gives me no great pleasure to tell you this."

"And what will you do once he takes power?"

"Honestly? I don't know," replied the Bear, momentarily removing his hand from the gear stick and stroking his chin thoughtfully. His other hand remained clasped tightly to the steering wheel with his elbow resting casually on the open window sill. Vitaly thought he looked very relaxed and genuinely unconcerned.

"Is your family still here? In Virubol?" asked Vitaly.

"No, they're all gone now," replied the Bear casually.

"Emigrated?"

"Dead," replied the Bear, turning to look Vitaly in the eye. "My father and brothers were killed in the civil war while fighting for the Reds."

"I'm sorry," replied Vitaly softly.

"Don't be," replied the Bear, looking away to take in the

roadway again. "They made their choice and I doubt they regret it."

"I assume then that you were a red?" asked Vitaly.

"Your assumption is correct, comrade," replied the Bear, unsmiling.

"And did you fight the Germans?"

"I did."

"When did you join the Bolsheviks?" asked Vitaly and the two men's eyes met again before the Bear quickly looked away.

"I didn't mutiny if that's what you're thinking," the Bear stated coolly.

"That's not what I meant, Anya. I was just curious."

"I left Russia between the abdication and the October Revolution."

"You left Russia? In your moment of glory?"

"Yes."

"But why?" asked Vitaly, confused.

The Bear hesitated before replying. Distracted, he drove the Fiat past a thick patch of pine and failed to see the large pothole lying in the road. The Fiat and its occupants were jolted violently, causing Vitaly to swear loudly in response to the pain.

"I'm sorry, comrade," said the Bear apologetically. "I didn't see that one."

"It's fine," hissed Vitaly as he cradled his leg tentatively.

"What did you ask me?" said the Bear.

"What? Oh yeah. Why did you leave Russia after the abdication? What could possibly be so important?"

"It was necessary for me to visit England," the Bear replied evasively.

"Why?" asked Vitaly, despite feeling intrusive.

The Bear turned to him again and gave him a stern look. Finally, Vitaly thought he had crossed the line.

"Any other Cheka, and you would be in trouble, comrade," the Bear replied very seriously before breaking into a smile and turning back to the road.

Relieved, Vitaly pushed on. "Why?"

"Why what?"

"Why did you visit England?"

"To visit my aunt and uncle."

After pausing to think about that statement, Vitaly spoke again. "I thought your family was dead?" he asked, careful to display the necessary sensitivity.

"Allow me to clarify: I have no family alive in Russia anymore," explained the Bear. "However, my uncle Robert and aunt Sydney live in England. London, to be precise."

"So, you're part English?"

"They are not blood relatives, merely family friends of my late parents who I refer to as aunt and uncle. When I left Virubol, it was to go and live with them in London."

"I understand," replied Vitaly, smiling. He couldn't help but be impressed. Not only was this man, who was only a few years older than himself, maybe five, a member of the Cheka, but he was also honest, trustworthy and well-travelled.

"I'm impressed, comrade Anya," stated Vitaly, nodding his head.

"It's not that impressive," replied the Bear. "But I'll take it regardless," he finished, chuckling with amusement.

"Your English must be excellent," stated Vitaly before the Bear reeled off several quick sentences in what he could only assume was perfect English. Personally, he understood very little but was still able to pick up a word here and there. He'd heard it spoken during the war but really, what did a peasant boy from Siberia need with English?

"Here we are, comrade," said the Bear with satisfaction as the trees ahead thinned and the road ascended a slight grade.

Finally, Vitaly recognised the location – he was home! It's likely he would've realised earlier but he'd been distracted by the Bear and engrossed in their conversation.

"Home, sweet, home." Stated the Bear as he slowed the Fiat down before coming to a stop outside the woven stick fence that enclosed the Borisov family's izba. Turning to his passenger, he smiled.

"I'm going to drop you here and head into Virubol to collect the doctor. Will you be able to walk to the door?" he asked over the noise of the idling engine.

"I'll be fine, comrade," replied Vitaly. "I'm grateful for everything you've done for me and my family," he exclaimed before offering the Bear his hand. "Thank you."

The Bear took hold of it then gently placed his other hand on top. "You're welcome, comrade," he replied.

After releasing Vitaly's hand, both men jumped in their seats as someone screamed "Vitaly!" from close by. They turned their heads in unison and looked in the direction of its source and observed Lena running around the side of the izba with Pyotr and comrade Kasaev following close behind.

"Vitaly!" she cried again, making her way through the gateway and around the Fiat to his door before reaching over and throwing her arms around her son.

"Mama," he muttered, muffled by her embrace.

"Vitaly! Oh, we were so worried!" she cried before planting several wet kisses on his forehead and cheeks.

"Mama, please, I'm okay," came his muffled reply.

"Here, let me look at you," she said, releasing him before taking hold of his face instead. "You're hurt!" she cried.

"Mama, please," begged Vitaly. "I'm okay. Tell her, Anya," he said, attempting to look at the Bear.

"Save for some bumps and bruises and of course the old leg injury, he's fine, Mrs Borisov," the Bear assured her.

"We were so worried, Vitaly!" explained Lena emotionally.

"I'm sorry, Mama," replied Vitaly. "If I hadn't lost my temper and hit Karasev none of this would have happened."

"Don't you worry about that now, Vitaly," interjected his father. "I figure Karasev deserved what he got, probably worse if what comrade Anya here told us is the truth."

"It is," replied the Bear, nodding his head with certainty and continuing to smile.

Exasperated, Pyotr said, "For goodness' sake, let him go, Lena," and he grabbed her arms and pulled them away from Vitaly's face. "He said he's okay."

"I just wanted to make sure, Pyotr," she replied, wiping away several tears.

"Is everything okay here, Kasaev?" the Bear asked his comrade.

"Yes boss," he replied. "They've been worried, obviously. The others arrived a couple of hours ago," he added, tilting his head in the direction of the izba to indicate the people standing there. Vitaly looked around and was both relieved and surprised to find his uncle, aunt and cousin standing just outside the izba's front gate smiling at him.

"Excellent," replied the Bear jovially. "As I just explained to Vitaly, I'm going to drop him here and head into Virubol to collect the doctor. Will you join me, Kasaev?"

"Sure thing, boss," Kasaev replied. "I think a little family time is in order and I don't wish to intrude," he added pleasantly before smiling from one Borisov to another.

"Very well then," exclaimed the Bear, tapping the steering wheel restlessly. "Can I help you indoors, Vitaly?"

"No, no, it's okay, Anya," replied Vitaly dismissively. "If necessary, Papa and uncle Anatoly can. But I should be okay to get from here to there," he said, pointing towards the izba before opening his door and swinging out his legs.

Ignoring the anguished facial expression of his mother, he stood up gingerly and closed the door behind him. "Thank you again, comrade," he stated, tilting his cap and reaching over to once again shake the Bears hand.

Finally, turning to face his parents, he smiled appreciatively as both his father and uncle placed supportive arms under his shoulders. Led by Lena, Irina and Sofia, he was carefully guided around the Fiat and through the gate before disappearing behind the izba.

The Bear, watching them go, couldn't held but wonder; How will Vitaly explain and reason with his family about the very real and looming threat of Joseph Stalin? He'd warned him for a reason. But would they listen? The Bear worried for the Borisov's. He worried for all of Russia.

"Boss, are we going?" interrupted Kasaev.

"What, Nikolai?" replied the Bear absentmindedly.

"The doctor? We need to collect the doctor, remember?" asked Kasaev.

The Bear, shaking his head, suddenly remembered what he was doing. "Yes, yes, the doctor. We had better go," he said. And with a sideways glance at Kasaev, who had somehow managed to enter the vehicle without the Bear noticing, he put the Fiat into gear and quickly accelerated away.

PRESENT DAY

"I never saw the Bear again after that day," exclaimed Tully thoughtfully, his eyes squinted as he looked out the window at the brightly setting sun. The glass containing his vodka remained full, although there had been several occasions during his story that he had reached for it and looked as if he was going to take a drink.

"So, you're Vitaly?" I asked with intrigue, my eyebrows raised. I'd had my suspicions.

Tully turned to look at me, his face expressionless. I searched it for a sign of confirmation and found a slight curl at the corner of his mouth. It was the thinnest trace of a smile.

"You figured it out then, John?" he asked me playfully before breaking into a smile.

"You just confirmed it for me," I replied, smiling back.

"And if I denied it, would you have believed me?"

"No, Tully, no I wouldn't have," I replied as his eyes bore into mine. They were twinkling. Was that the twinkle of mischievousness?

"And may I ask why?"

"Well, um, for starters that story you just told me is exceptionally detailed," I replied. "So, you've either recited it hundreds of times or you have the book," I added, looking around quickly for said literature.

Smiling, he replied, "That doesn't confirm anything. Also, if any one of these Western police shows have taught me anything, I believe that's called circumstantial evidence." We both laughed.

"No, I suppose it doesn't," I replied, clearing my throat. "However, you stated that was the last time you saw the Bear," I added with satisfaction.

"True, John, true. But, could it not have been the Bear who told me this story?" he asked. I paused again and thought about my reply. I was confused, I admit. Why would he deny being the protagonist?

"Your statement in regards to that being the last time you saw the Bear indicates you were there, which you yourself reinforce," I replied slowly, carefully thinking my way through my answer. "If you never saw the Bear again, how could he have told it to you subsequently?"

His smile widened at my reply. "This is why I like you, John," he stated affectionately. "You're bright and can think."

Despite feeling slightly embarrassed by the compliment, I replied, "well, thank you, Tully. Am I to understand then that I am right in my deduction?"

"You are correct, John," he replied jovially.

"So, your real name is Vitaly?" I asked with intrigue and again raised my eyebrows.

"Vitaly Petrovich Borisov, born November 17th, 1898 in Virubol, Siberia. I changed my name, anglicised it, after I emigrated to Australia in 1933," he added.

"To Tully George Bradman?" I asked, smiling. I'd read his

name a thousand times before. It was written on his medical chart and was displayed in bold on the board above his bed.

"Yes, yes, I know," he replied lightly. "You're wondering how I arrived at that collection?"

"Well, yes," I replied, amused.

"I imagine the Tully part is obvious to you, John."

"Yes, I understood that part immediately," I replied. "I was more curious as to how you arrived on George and Bradman?"

"I didn't leave Siberia straight for Australia, John," he replied seriously before following with a short silence. "I first emigrated to England, a few years after the warning from the Bear. As he predicted, Lenin died and Stalin took power. The first of his warnings had come to fruition."

"How long did you remain in Russia?"

"I left Siberia in 1927, absent all of my family. They remained unconvinced despite my warnings, and paid for it in the end."

"I'm sorry," I stated apprehensively but he waved my apology away.

"It's in the past, John, all in the past. Anyway, I boarded a steamer in Archangel that sailed on to Denmark and then into Middlesbrough, England, where I spent the interim years employed by Dorman Long, the steel manufacturer," he explained. "I managed to remain employed there during the Depression and by 1932, sick of the weather and having saved enough pounds, I packed up and boarded another steamer for Australia via the Suez Canal, arriving at Station Pier in Melbourne about a month and a half later to begin my new life." He smiled with happiness at the recollection.

"It wasn't until I began living and working in Australia that I adopted the name. In England I'd been called Ruski because I was Russian, which evolved into being called Rusty, which I didn't mind. The name George however was borrowed from the king of England at the time, George V, who'd been a Russian ally and cousin to our former Czar. As for Bradman, well, I thought that would be obvious, wouldn't it, John?" he asked cheekily.

After thinking about the question, with pursed lips, I shook my head then shrugged my shoulders in defeat. "You win. Why Bradman?" I asked, watching as his eyes twinkled yet again.

"John, John, John, John, John," he said playfully, shaking his head with mock disappointment. "What did I just praise you for?"

"Um," I stuttered in reply.

"Your ability to think, my friend," he replied.

"Okay, okay. Bradman, Bradman, Bradman," I recited, thinking about the significance. As if instinctively, my mind wandered to the newspaper Tully had shown me earlier.

"Take your time, John," interrupted Tully, goading me.

Frowning, I ignored him and continued to think. The front page had mentioned the fall of the Soviet Union, but how did that have anything to do with Bradman? Then I remembered mentioning the cricket and suddenly, it dawned on me and I finally arrived at the answer. "Don Bradman? The cricketer?" I asked brightly.

"Correct!" He beamed, clapping his hands together again.

"I would never have thought a Russian would've liked cricket."

"I was never a huge fan, John, but you're forgetting that I lived in England for four to five years, which coincided with Bradman's rise to prominence. The English are cricket mad and it helps to know at least a little about the game when you live and work around so many fanatics. Engaging the other iron workers in conversation about Bradman was how I mastered the English language. It was football that taught me the expletives," he finished, chuckling.

"Yes, I can appreciate that, Tully," I said, laughing. Becoming serious again, my curiosity got the better of me and I dared to ask a more personal question. "I completely understand if you don't want to answer, but do you know what happened to your family?"

Tully stared back at me, the twinkle in his eyes disappearing. His smile faded and he reached down for his vodka. Picking up the glass, he placed it to his lips and opened his mouth before throwing back its entirety in one go. Swallowing, he looked at me, sadness now having spread across his face. Then he spoke.

"Okay, John," he said, softly and emotionally. "Choosing to remain in Russia under Stalin, my family fell victim to the Great Purge," he stated shakily. "The Red Terror had been bad but paled in comparison in both scope and sheer numbers. My cousin Sofia's husband Edgar had been a Jew, which marked him and Sofia and their children. I believe, and I don't have all the facts, nor do I believe I ever will, that her parents and mine tried to protect and hide them, which marked them also," he explained as I sat there horrified. "It's possible that uncle Anatoly, aunt Irina and my parents merely stood in their way; either way, they were eliminated for it," he finished bitterly.

"I'm sorry, Tully," I replied awkwardly. *What are you meant to say to that?*

"Again, John, it's okay," he replied with another appreciative smile before placing his empty glass back on the table.

Changing the subject, I said, "I've always thought your English is good."

Tully, beaming, replied with enthusiasm, "Thank you! Learning English is one of my proudest achievements! Of course, I understand that it can still be difficult to understand me through my accent."

"I get by," I replied with a smile.

"That you do, John, that you do," he replied, returning my smile. "And thank you for that change of subject." He nodded appreciatively. "But returning to my story, is there not another question you want to ask?"

"Uh, I uh, I suppose," I mumbled, thinking. "Yes! What happened to Karasev and his Soviet buddies?"

Tully looked disappointed at the question, leaving me with the impression there was another, more pressing one I'd not yet asked. Regardless, he replied, "I never saw them again either but unlike the Bear, I wasn't disappointed."

I nodded, then abruptly changing the subject again, I asked, "What did you do once you arrived in Melbourne?" In response, he smiled encouragingly.

"Using my improved English, I secured employment at the Carlton and United Brewery in Abbotsford as a general labourer," he explained in reply. "Within a couple of years, I became an apprentice fitter and turner and remained so until I retired in 1964. My very first pay slip was handed to me by my wife," he chuckled.

"Really!?"

"Audrey Grace Bradley," he replied softly, glancing out the window again at the slowly setting sun. "Now she was a lady! But goodness could she keep the men in line!" He chuckled in reminiscence. "Not that she had to. Jock McHale was a manager and all the Collingwood boys were employed there and smart enough not to upset him out of fear of missing out on playing in a premiership."

"Jock McHale?" I asked. "The famous coach of Collingwood?"

"One and the same," replied Tully, nodding enthusiastically. "I'm a lifelong Magpies fan because of him and the boys. Not that you had much choice, working there. I remember a South Melbourne player coming to work there and the next year transferring to Collingwood." We both laughed.

"Grace was a decade younger than me and had moved down to Melbourne from here, Castlemaine," he explained, much to my surprise. "I can't help but imagine what her parents thought when she told them she was dating a Russian émigré," he chuckled again.

"So that's how you ended up here in town!"

"Correct. Although we stayed in Melbourne until, what was it, 1970, I think. I can't remember precisely."

"That's okay, Tully. Go on."

"Grace always wanted to come home," he continued, sadness creeping into his voice. "Her father passed, which left her mother alone. We moved back so she could care for her and she ended up getting sick herself. We never had kids and Grace, like me, was an only child so when her mum died, and then she died, I was left all alone. It wasn't long afterwards that I ended up here at Alexander."

As I sat there across from him, our eyes met and I shook my head in disbelief at his story. From a small rural Siberian village through a world war, a revolution and two emigrations to a small room on the Tolstrup ward at the Mount Alexander Hospital in Castlemaine, Victoria, Australia. Believe me when I say, I was fascinated! Then again, many of the residents here had fascinating tales. We had several war veterans, from both the first and second World Wars, one of whom had been a bomber pilot in the RAF who'd later emigrated in the sixties as one of the famous ten-pound poms.

"I am fascinated, Tully. Genuinely fascinated," I stated, continuing to shake my head. "But I find myself continuously getting distracted. Not that I didn't want to hear all of that. I can assure you I did and am grateful for you sharing it with me, after all this time." I smiled and nodded to him affectionately.

"You have another question, John?" he asked, as if he knew what I wanted to know.

"Well, yes," I replied before smiling suspiciously.

"Ask away then, John," he replied.

I hesitated, curious as to whether he knew what my question would be. Then I asked, "And what of the Romanovs?" and Tully's face lit up, confirming my suspicion.

"I have spent a considerable amount of time since our meeting that day in the clearing in the woods researching the former Czar and his family and I'm certain it was them," he stated with conviction.

"You don't believe it was a dream, a hallucination, alcohol or the effects of concussion then?" I asked cautiously.

"I have always been able to tell the difference between a dream and reality," he replied very seriously. "This, this was something else," he added, waving his index finger at me. "Something different and far too real."

"How can you tell?" I asked.

"I collected photographs of the family and while the other three sisters or daughters' faces remain somewhat vague to me, Nicholas or Feliks' face and Maria or Marta's are identical to those photographs," he replied. "Maria's eyes are not easily forgotten, nor replicated," he added before becoming momentarily hypnotised by the memory.

Refocusing, he continued, "I've also read copiously about both their individual physical and personality descriptions and would have to say, they're a match."

"Do you believe the imposters?" I asked.

"Hmm, I'm suspicious, John," he replied, frowning. "Lenin was a clever man. He allowed the reports of the Czar's execution to be released in the newspapers shortly afterwards. The safety and wellbeing of the rest of the Imperial Family was left deliberately vague, I suspect because they were murdered, which is an unsettling thought considering as I stated only a few moments ago, I firmly believe I met them, minus the Czarina and Czarevich that is," he finished, stroking his chin thoughtfully.

"Perhaps they weren't murdered then?" I asked tentatively. "For one, if Feliks was Nicholas, how could he have been murdered? Maria told you that they escaped and that the Latvian guards had shot and killed the Bolshevik ones."

"I know! I've just about sent myself crazy rationalising and theorising, John. It does me no good to dwell on it anymore. It makes my heart feel like it's tied up in a knot. I know this, though: that night I spent with Maria felt as real as any one of the thousands subsequent nights I spent with Grace. I know that might sound disrespectful to my wife but that's not my intention..."

"Let me assure you Tully, that's not the way I interpreted it," I replied reassuringly.

"Well, thank you for that," he replied, relieved. "Although it doesn't stop the feeling of guilt."

From his response, another person came to mind and I became disgusted with myself for not thinking of him earlier. But what could I do but offer reassurance? "Evgeny's not your fault, Tully," I stated firmly, looking him straight in the eye.

"Survivor's guilt. Survivor's guilt is what they call it, John," he stated with resignation. "Another thing I've dwelt on over the years. I've often thought that if I hadn't cried out, Evgeny wouldn't have stopped and turned and taken the brunt of that shell. But then, if he'd continued on, I would've copped it and been killed instead and him spared, destined to spend our lives in the reverse of the other," he finished, our eye contact lingering as I shook my head, lost for words.

"I often think it's ironic," he stated, smiling sheepishly.

"What's that, Tully?" I asked uncertainly.

"That Evgeny, who I mercilessly teased for being a coward, was killed being brave whilst I, who prided himself on being brave, was spared due to an act of cowardice."

"That's an awfully harsh assessment, Tully."

"An accurate one though!" he replied, before looking down at his feet in shame.

We sat in silence for the next minute or so, both in thought but about different things. Another question came to mind, one I had overlooked until now.

"What happened to the egg?" I asked uncertainly before our eyes met again.

"I kept it, John. All of these years I kept it," he replied, maintaining a serious expression. I looked around, half expecting to see it sitting idle on the window sill or his bedside table. I'd known and cared for him for the last ten years and never seen anything that resembled a Fabergé egg.

"Where?" I asked with trepidation.

"Open my wardrobe and you'll find on the floor underneath my suitcase a small steel box with a combination lock," he explained. "Go on," he said, smiling at me encouragingly.

I rose from my seat and walked over to the wardrobe before I took the handle and pulled. Hanging up inside were a dozen shirts, approximately the same number of jumpers and at least a half dozen pair of trousers. I looked down before crouching down and investigated the drawers which I found filled with his underwear and socks. Continuing on, I inspected the spaces for his shoes of which he owned only two pairs. Below was a cavity that held a stack of books and resting on top, almost touching the underside of the shelf above, his suitcase. I turned my head and looked at him.

"The box is in the middle of that stack of books on the bottom left-hand side under the suitcase," he stated assuredly, pointing from his seat. I turned back and using my hands, I began to feel my way up the stack and quickly found what I was looking for.

"You can move whatever you need to move, John. Put it on the bed if you like," Tully stated, a touch of excitement noticeable in his voice.

I slid the suitcase out and swung it up and onto his bed. Then I grabbed the pile of books and carefully placed them next to the suitcase. When I let them go, they slid over and spread out across the bed.

"Never mind them, John," interrupted Tully.

Heeding his advice, I crouched back down and collected the steel box. It was cool to the touch and surprisingly heavy. I stood up and turned around to find Tully sitting forward in his seat expectantly. "That's it!" he said excitedly as I carried it over and placed it on the table in front of him. "Would you close the door please, John?" he asked.

"Yeah, no problem," I replied compliantly. I turned and walked over to the door and shut it before I rejoined Tully, returning to my seat in anticipation.

He looked me in the eye with an intensity I hadn't seen before. It was as if he was X-raying me. Then he spoke. "John, you can open it," he remarked casually before sitting back in the chair leisurely. My face must've shown my surprise because he chuckled and smiled back at me knowingly.

"I had the same experience," he said, nodding. "You just wait until you see what's inside," he added with a wide grin which somehow revealed all of his teeth. I looked down at the box and fiddled around with it restlessly, then back up at Tully.

"What's the code?" I asked, whispering instinctively. Somehow, I felt like I was doing something wrong.

"One, four, zero, six," replied Tully very seriously. I doubt he felt any such reservations as I did. In fact, I suspected he felt relief, as if he was unburdening himself of a great secret.

"Is that number significant?" I asked as I begun spinning the dials displaying the numbers into place.

"It is Maria's Romanovs birthday," he replied as I met his eyes, which displayed a continued intensity. "The 14th of June, 1899."

I looked down at the dial and hesitated. "One, four, zero, six," I repeated, straining with concentration. Surely this can't be real? I asked myself before I commenced counting down and begun slowly spinning the last dial into place. Nine, eight, seven and finally with a loud click, six. Lifting the lid, I gently folded it back and revealed its contents.

A Parting Gift

A dark purple silk pouch with gold-threaded drawstrings rested nestled between sheets of crumpled-up newspaper which held it in place. In disbelief, I immediately met Tully's eyes again and this time found them twinkling brightly as an amused grin crossed his face.

"No way," I said to him through an uncertain smile.

He remained silent, his grin widening as he nodded his head.

"No way," I repeated, unable to look away.

"Open it," he replied softly. "Go on."

I shook my head, careful not to break eye contact. This had to be some sort of joke, I thought to myself. There was no way this could be real. But I broke eye contact regardless and looking down at the purple silk pouch, I reached into the box and withdrew it.

Whatever was inside was heavy and egg-shaped, perhaps confirming what I thought to be untrue. I could feel through the pouch that the item inside had bulges along its exterior that were solid to the touch.

"Come along, John, I'm ninety-three, and at this rate will be dead before you get to see what's inside," interrupted Tully teasingly.

Without looking up, I chuckled at his joke and shook my head again in disbelief. Carefully, I pulled the thread of one of the loops and they both came undone. I cautiously opened the pouch before reaching inside and taking hold of the egg. It was wrapped inside a silk cloth or kerchief. After withdrawing it, I placed the now empty pouch down on the table before slowly unwrapping it.

Dazzling! If there is one word that accurately describes the sight before my eyes it's dazzling. In the palm of my hand rested a Fabergé egg. Something I'd never thought I'd ever hold. Its many jewels iridescently reflecting the abundant light within the room.

I rotated it slowly in my hand, admiring it from every angle. As described, the immediate and most notable feature was its diamond-set Cupid's arrows symbolizing Love. The crafting was beyond impressive, with multi-coloured gold and decorations of bands of rose-cut diamonds and coverings of translucent red guilloché enamel. The miniature portrait of a young Emperor Czar Nicholas II was there too under a table-cut diamond and at its base the date 1894.

"Holy shit, it's real!" I exclaimed, looking up and meeting Tully's eyes. He smiled broadly back at me and nodded his head gently. He looked like he might even cry.

"I can't believe it, Tully," I stated. "I really can't believe what I'm holding!"

"Nor could I, at the time," he replied softly, his voice wavering.

"How have you managed to keep this secret all this time?" I asked.

"With relative ease actually," he replied casually. "Secrets are easy to keep when you don't share them with anyone," he added, a little solemnly. I looked at him and felt a twang of pity.

"Did Grace, your wife, did she know?" I asked.

"Oh yes," he replied brightly. "She was the first person I ever told. Not even my mother and father knew, which in retrospect was amazing, considering we all lived in that tiny izba."

"Why didn't you tell them?" I asked, a little shocked. Meanwhile I kept rotating the egg in my hand, admiring its beauty.

"The Bear told me not to tell anyone," he replied defensively. "And I don't think they would've believed it was real if I had, plus, not that they would deliberately betray me, but I convinced myself I was protecting them by not sharing that information as the Bear had advised," he explained, as I nodded along, having managed to take my eye off the egg for a few seconds.

"What did Grace think? Did she believe you?" I asked.

"Initially I think she thought I was crazy," he replied, amused.

"Yeah?" I asked, laughing.

"In her defence, I told her the story first before showing her the egg, much like you," he continued. "Unlike you, however, she thought I was talking absolute nonsense and having a laugh at her expense."

"You managed to talk her round though?"

"Yes, but it took some convincing," he replied jovially before quickly looking out the window and then back at me. "I remember it clearly. She was far less interested in the egg than my romantic tryst with this mysterious Maria."

"Oh, she thought?" I asked, having quickly understood the implication.

"Yes, she thought!" he replied, cutting me off before laughing. "That's why it took some convincing. Of course, I hadn't so the conversation got back on track and the revelation was forthcoming."

"And what did she think?" I asked.

"She couldn't believe it either! Of course, she wanted confirmation and suggested taking it to a local jeweller and having them ascertain it. I didn't want that though," he added with a sudden surliness.

"Why?" I asked curiously.

"Well, firstly, the Bear had told me not to and I figured revealing its existence would be dangerous even in Australia," he explained in reply, having suddenly become deadly serious. "If I took it in, the jeweller would probably report it and pass that on to the relative authorities, who would then have tracked me down."

"I see," I replied.

"And," he continued, "I would be questioned and possibly interrogated about where and the circumstances under which I obtained it. You know as well as I do that that's not any ordinary jewel!" He pointed at the egg held securely in my hand. "So, I never did and I stand by that decision, especially after Trotsky was assassinated in Mexico a couple of years later. Stalin had him killed, and Stalin would want that back," he explained, pointing again at the egg. "And fuck him, he wasn't getting it back after she gave it to me, more or less, anyways," he added passionately.

A short silence followed as Tully watched me slowly rotate the egg in my hand and marvel at how the light in the room was caught and reflected by its many jewels. Then another question popped into my head.

"Did you ever go back to the clearing?" I asked, pulling my eyes from the egg and placing them firmly on Tully once again.

"I looked," he replied, sadly. "I looked several times in fact."

"But you never found it?"

With resignation, he replied, "No. No, I never did," and shook his head. "I tried retracing my steps through the woods and the route the Bear drove us. All I can concretely remember about the car trip was the pain, the conversation with the Bear, or more specifically his warnings, and the confusion I felt," he explained, following it with a great sigh. "It's frustrating."

"I can imagine," I replied. "It's a shame though," I continued. "Did you ever wonder if that grave actually contained more Romanov treasure?"

"I believe the proof lies in the existence and my possession of that egg, John," replied Tully, again pointing to it. "But who knows? I know I never will for certain."

"Hmm," I said. "Perhaps with the fall, things will come to light," I stated, hopefully.

"I doubt it, John," replied Tully sullenly. "Russians are secretive by nature."

Another silence followed his statement but I could sense he had more to say. I know I had a myriad of questions but none jumped out as particularly prescient at this moment.

"Why don't you open it, and take a look inside, John?" asked Tully. "That little latch will open it."

I turned the egg in my hand and found the latch. It clicked, springing open a millimetre or two. I pushed the top half of the egg up and open and looked inside. Within was a small bejewelled replica of the Imperial crown and a ruby drop. Once again, dazzling is the word that comes to mind to describe what I saw. I lifted them out carefully and using my opposite hand, placed the open egg down in the security of my lap.

I placed the replica crown and drop into the palm of my now empty hand and admired them. Using the index finger of my free hand I gently touched and rubbed the jewels, feeling the smoothness of the drop and the jaggedness of the diamonds set into the miniature crown. That's when Tully broke the silence.

"I have a question for you now, John," he stated.

Meeting his eye, I replied, "Fire away, Tully," and flashed him a smile.

"Would you like it?" he asked me.

Confused, I immediately assumed I'd misheard him and asked, "Do I like it?" and followed up with, "Of course! It's beautiful."

"No, no, John," replied Tully, shaking his head. "Would you like it?" he asked again and this time I didn't misunderstand. I sat there transfixed, certain that he wasn't being serious. He beamed at me and nodded his head reassuringly.

"Would I like it?" I asked in reply, dumbfounded.

"That's correct," replied Tully very seriously.

"You can't be serious? I uh, I can't accept this," I mumbled, shaking my head.

"I'm not talking about taking it into your possession right now, John, but when I die it's yours," he replied.

"What?" I stammered, still uncertain of what was happening.

"Let me explain," he replied. "You can relax, it's okay," he assured me. "I'm an old man. My memory's going, my mind too. Who knows how many years I have left. I have no family, few if any friends, living at least, and you've been kind and generous to me consistently over the last decade. You've introduced me to your children and brought them in to visit me on more than one occasion. Now, that mightn't seem like much to you, but that's a hell of a lot to me and I guess what I'm trying to say is, you've become somewhat like a son to me and I regard you as such," he finished, his eyes displaying that familiar twinkle.

"Tully," I exclaimed very seriously before quickly being cut off.

"No, John, no, you've earned this. Actually, no, you deserve this," he stated almost pleadingly. "And I have no one else to give it to."

"Well, I uh, I, thank you Tully," I replied very ineloquently, smiling at the kind old man. "That means a lot," I added, my gaze finding his straightened, injured and badly scarred leg that stretched out straight in front of him while the other bent at the knee forming a ninety-degree angle with the floor. The image caused me to smile again.

"So, you will take it?" he asked. "Upon my death of course," he added, beaming.

"How can I say no to that?" I replied, beaming in return.

He clapped his hands together and rose with surprising speed and grace from his chair before rounding the table and coming to a halt next to me. He extended his arms expectantly and I quickly placed the jewels and egg on the table and rose to embrace him.

Our embrace lasted for more than a minute. I didn't fight it. Before letting go, he whispered into my ear, "Thank you," and we separated. Patting me on the shoulder, he spoke again. "All I ask is, like the Bear advised me and now I advise you is, please don't sell it, give it away or reveal it to anyone with the exception of your children, perhaps when they're a little older, and your beautiful wife."

"I promise I won't do any of those things," I replied automatically, causing him to smile at me warmly.

"Good, John. I wish to spare you the circus that would follow," he explained.

"I understand," I replied before asking, "How much do you think it's worth?"

"Millions," he replied, brightly.

"Wow," was all I could muster in response as I blinked stupidly. Tully laughed at my reaction.

"Goodness, John, I've kept you far too long," he stated, turning away to look at the clock upon the wall. "You should be getting home to that lovely family of yours and not wasting your time sitting here and listening to the ramblings of an old man."

"It's been my pleasure, Tully," I replied warmly.

"Mine too," he replied, turning back to look at me. "Now don't worry, I'll pack this up," he stated, pointing to the jewels and glasses on the table and then the suitcase and books piled on his bed. "You just be on your way."

"It is late," I replied, looking at the clock. "Thank you again," I stated, stepping forward and shaking his hand. "I'll see you in a couple of days I suppose."

"I'll be here!" he replied jovially and I turned away and headed for the door before another question popped into my mind.

Turning back to face him, I asked, "What are your thoughts on Bolshevism these days, Tully?"

He looked at me thoughtfully before answering. "Do you know the difference between socialism and communism?"

"No, I don't think so," I replied quickly before taking a moment to consider it. "I mean, socialism is better, right?"

He took a moment to consider my question then replied, "Yes. Socialism is better, but socialism is the equal distribution of poverty whereas communism is nothing but socialism with a gun at your back," he replied with conviction. "And judging by today's paper," he looked over to the folded paper resting on his bedside table, "I'd say the Russian people, and more broadly, all of the former Soviet people, have finally had enough of the gun in their back," he finished, offering me a blank look.

"That would have to be Churchill?" I asked, impressed.

"That's correct, John," he replied.

"One more question, and I swear this is the last one," I stated, receiving an encouraging smile. "Do you still dream about her? Maria?"

"Occasionally, yes," he replied, his smile widening. "Still as vividly as I did seventy years ago."

I nodded my head in understanding and flashed him a final smile before turning again and exiting through the door.

The chronology of events after I left his room, I can't be certain of, but I like to imagine Tully, after returning all of those items he had just mentioned to their rightful places, had returned to his seat by the window and watched the sun slowly set on another day in his very long life, perhaps accompanied by another vodka.

I'm certain he was happy, unburdened, and spent the last hours of sunlight reminiscing about his late wife, Maria and his visit to that little izba in the clearing in the woods. That thought and the image of him sitting there bathed in the late afternoon sunlight has managed to leave a smile on my face at every recollection for the last thirty years.

It doesn't hurt either, being able to put your hands on a jewel-encrusted egg that somehow manages to sparkle even in a darkened room, drawing the light out of even the darkest of places.

THE END

Acknowledgments

There are several people who directly contributed to this book in some way and while I'm unsure about other people's inspiration when it comes to writing, mine initially came from my co-worker Damo who complimented me on an email I sent approximately eighteen months ago. Pretty random right? His encouraging words not only sparked my interest in writing but also gave me the belief I could do so.

Damien Harrison (mentioned above), Andrew Lewis, Rita Revell, Anthony Montinaro, Katey Ansell, Gary Van Den Driesen, Dean Clinton Hartshorn, Deanna Norris and Wendy Entwisle all took the time out of their busy lives to read my story which, considering at that time it hadn't even been professionally copyedited, is even more impressive and appreciated. Their feedback, suggestions, encouragement and criticism has been invaluable to me and was an integral step in this process. Thank you, guys!

Copyediting was completed by Tom Feltham who I linked with on the website Reedsy. His skill at ironing out my mistakes was essential. He's also been an invaluable source of advice throughout the process having worked in the industry for years. Sorry about all the questions Tom but thank you for always replying.

Arjan Van Woensel, who I also linked with on Reedsy, undertook the herculean task of both designing my book and providing the typesetting. From cover to cover he was able to recreate and give life to an image I had in my mind. Take a good look at the front cover and tell me you're not impressed! Thank you Arjan!

www.ingramcontent.com/pod-product-compliance
Lightning Source LLC
LaVergne TN
LVHW011417080426
835512LV00005B/101